PERGAMON INSTITUTE OF ENGLISH (OXFORD)

English Language Teaching Documents

General Editor: C. J. BRUMFIT

TEACHING LITERATURE OVERSEAS
LANGUAGE-BASED APPROACHES

The British Council ELT Documents — Back Issues

See also:

Michael Cummings and Robert Simmons
The Language of Literature, 1983

TEACHING LITERATURE OVERSEAS
LANGUAGE-BASED APPROACHES

Edited by

C. J. BRUMFIT
University of London Institute of Education

ELT Documents 115

Published in association with

THE BRITISH COUNCIL

by

PERGAMON PRESS

Oxford · New York · Toronto · Sydney · Paris · Frankfurt

U.K.	Pergamon Press Ltd., Headington Hill Hall, Oxford OX3 0BW, England
U.S.A.	Pergamon Press Inc., Maxwell House, Fairview Park, Elmsford, New York 10523, U.S.A.
CANADA	Pergamon Press Canada Ltd., Suite 104, 150 Consumers Road, Willowdale, Ontario M2J 1P9, Canada
AUSTRALIA	Pergamon Press (Aust.) Pty. Ltd., P.O. Box 544, Potts Point, N.S.W. 2011, Australia
FRANCE	Pergamon Press SARL, 24 rue des Ecoles, 75240 Paris, Cedex 05, France
FEDERAL REPUBLIC OF GERMANY	Pergamon Press GmbH, Hammerweg 6, D-6242 Kronberg-Taunus, Federal Republic of Germany

First edition 1983

Library of Congress Cataloging in Publication Data

Main entry under title:
Teaching literature overseas.
(English language teaching documents; 115)
Includes index.
1. English language—Study and teaching—Foreign countries—Addresses, essays, lectures. 2. English language—Study and teaching—Foreign speakers—Addresses, essays, lectures.
I. Brumfit, Christopher. II. Title. III. Series.
PR37.T4 1983   820′.7   83-8277

British Library Cataloguing in Publication Data

Teaching literature overseas: language-based approaches.—(ELT documents; 115)
1. English literature—Study and teaching—foreign students
I. Brumfit, C. J.
820′.7   PR35
ISBN 0-08-030341-2

*Printed and bound in Great Britain by
Redwood Burn Ltd, Trowbridge, Wiltshire*

EDITOR'S PREFACE

This collection is here reprinted exactly as received from the British Council, except that a paper by Henry Widdowson has been added. Professor Widdowson was approached originally when this collection was being planned, but did not at that stage have time to offer anything. Since there has been a longer delay than expected between the writing and publication of these papers, it has proved possible to include one of his previously unpublished papers. In spite of the delay, however, this remains a timely collection, for the teaching of literature is increasingly being discussed by teachers of English, whether they come from linguistic or literary backgrounds.

C. J. Brumfit

ACKNOWLEDGEMENTS

Thanks are due to the following publishers, authors and literary agents for permission to quote from works in copyright:

Bolt & Watson Ltd: D. J. Enright *Memoirs of a Mendicant Professor*.

Jonathan Cape Ltd: James Joyce *A Portrait of the Artist as a Young Man, Stephen Hero*.

Chatto & Windus Ltd and C. K. Scott Moncrieff: Marcel Proust *Remembrance of Things Past*, translated by C. K. Scott Moncrieff.

E. P. Dutton and Company Inc. (USA): A. A. Milne *Winnie-the-Pooh*.

Faber & Faber Ltd: Ezra Pound 'In a Station of the Metro'; Ted Hughes 'Prometheus on his Crag'.

Granada Publishing Ltd: E. E. Cummings *Complete Poems*; R. S. Thomas *Selected Poems*.

Harcourt Brace Jovanovitch Inc. (USA): E. E. Cummings *Complete Poems 1913–1962*; Virginia Woolf *The Years*.

Harper & Row Ltd (USA): Ted Hughes 'Prometheus on his Crag'.

Heinemann Educational Books Ltd: Romanus Egudu and Donatus Nwoga *Igbo Traditional Verse*.

David Higham Associates Ltd: Dylan Thomas 'Ears in the Turrets Hear'; Wynford Vaughan-Thomas 'Hiraeth in NW3'.

Hill & Wang (Farrar, Straus & Giroux Inc.) (USA): Roland Barthes *Elements of Semiology*.

Hogarth Press Ltd and Virginia Woolf Literary Estate: Virginia Woolf *The Years*.

Houghton Mifflin Co. (USA): John Betjeman *Collected Poems*.

Longman Group Ltd: H. Fraser and W. R. O'Donnell *Applied Linguistics and the Teaching of English*.

McClelland & Stewart Ltd (Canada): A. A. Milne *Winnie-the-Pooh*.

Methuen & Co. Ltd: Terence Hawkes *Structuralism and Semiotics*.

Methuen Children's Books Ltd: A. A. Milne *Winnie-the-Pooh*.

John Murray (Publishers) Ltd: John Betjeman *Collected Poems*.

New Directions Publishing Corporation (USA): Ezra Pound 'In a Station of the Metro'; Dylan Thomas 'Ears in the Turrets Hear'; William Carlos Williams *Collected Earlier Poems*.

New Statesman: Desmond Skirrow 'Ode on a Grecian Urn Summarized'.

Nwamife Publishers Ltd (Nigeria): Romanus Egudu and Donatus Nwoga *Igbo Traditional Verse*.

Peter Owen Ltd: T. Connolly (ed.) *Joyce's Portrait*.

Ted Pauker: 'A Grouchy Goodnight to the Academic Year'.

A. D. Peters & Co. Ltd: Evelynm Waugh *Officers and Gentlemen*.

Random House Inc. (USA): Marcel Proust *Remembrance of Things Past*, translated by C. K. Scott Moncrief.
Scott Meredith Literary Agency Inc. (USA): P. G. Wodehouse 'To William (Whom We Have Missed)', 'The Gourmet's Love Song'.
Martin Secker & Warburg Ltd: Phyllis McGinley *Times Three*.
The Society of Authors: James Joyce *Stephen Hero*.
Wynford Vaughan-Thomas: 'Hiraeth in NW3'.
Viking Penguin Inc. (USA): James Joyce *A Portrait of the Artist as a Young Man*; Phyllis McGinley *Times Three*.
A. P. Watt Ltd and the Estate of Sir P. G. Wodehouse: P. G. Wodehouse 'To William (Whom We Have Missed)', 'The Gourmet's Love Song'.

CONTENTS

Discourse analysis. Literary stylistics. Application of linguistics to particular genres. Statistical studies. Semiology. Teaching. Some traditional approaches to style. Periodicals.

INTRODUCTION

NEIL GILROY-SCOTT

British Council, Pretoria

Few would dispute that there has been a decline in the prestige of English Literature study abroad, particularly in the context of language learning. Since 1945 language teaching theory has drawn attention to the inadequacies of literature-based methods in promoting the acquisition of language skills. It has been correctly pointed out that all too often emphasis on literary knowledge disguised poor language attainments — 'the maxi-coat of literature hiding the mini-skirt of language' (Arthur King). The trend has been to reduce, if not eliminate, the literature component at early and intermediate levels and to concentrate on reading, written and spoken skills. It is often still assumed that mastery of the language, as it is understood by the dominant teaching philosophies, will eventually produce, amongst other things, a supply of students capable of pursuing the advanced academic study of literature.

This is manifestly not the case. The picture emerging from overseas institutions is of increasing numbers of new students lacking both the background and the necessary study skills. There is an immediate need for guidance over the question of how to introduce students to the primary texts of literature from which they have so far been protected, and how to teach the strategies and study habits to enable them to cope with the heavy reading requirements in most tertiary level courses. In the long term the problem is the rehabilitation and reintegration of literature as an integral part of communicative language programmes not only to minimize the shock of such sudden and demanding exposure to primary texts, but also to exploit the enormously high potential of literature for educational enrichment.

Thus the papers in this collection are intended to promote discussion and experiment in what has so far been a much neglected field. They tend to focus more on the application of language studies to literature and this reflects the general prominence given to literary stylistics in recent years. Much less has been written on the use of authentic literary texts for language learning, but there are signs that developments in communicative language teaching will do much to remove the theoretical objections which have so far reduced its role to minimal proportions.

Literature teachers have responded to the influx of underprepared students in a variety of ways. There is still considerable faith in the efficacy of modern integrated language programmes and sophisticated language labs. If their language is inadequate then let them follow an intensive preparatory course of language study in their first year, the argument goes. Only then should they face the terrors of 'real' literature. Another response is to draw attention to the socio-cultural difficulties of the student in facing a foreign literature. The argument now is that you cannot understand Shakespeare without first knowing the seventeenth-century background, or more trivially that you cannot understand a certain Wordsworth poem if you have never seen a daffodil.

Both responses have led to what looks suspiciously like an escape from the text, or at least an attempt in the one case to postpone, in the other to minimize contact with the original text. It seems likely that the current emphasis on academic knowledge about texts, the dependence on critical authority, the popularity of 'bazaar' notes, and the enthusiasm for background courses are to a great extent the result of an underlying sense of inadequacy in face of the text. Students do not know how to approach the text and teachers do not know how to present it. Courses on the sociology, psychology, and history of literature and criticism proliferate which, while hopefully improving the reader's ability to comprehend the text, have the effect of separating him yet further from it. The academic cycle of lecture, printed critical authority, and examinations is the mark of authoritarian, fact-centred modes of learning, and it all seems very far removed from what one might loosely refer to as the 'original' purpose of literature.

What one regards as the 'purpose' of literature will very much depend on where one comes from and the place and status of literature in that country. But within the range of instruction and delight, the cognitive and affective aspects of reading, there will be broad agreement that literary texts are written to be read mainly by individuals in the privacy of their own homes, sometimes by consenting groups in public, and that something of the cognitive or affective or both should happen to the minds of those so exposed.

Clearly a movement is needed to re-establish the proper and basic relationship between the reader and the text and to make such activity a recognizable part of the educational structure. Anyone who has studied literature in a formal way will recognize that what happens when reading a set text is not the same as when reading the latest novel by Malcolm Bradbury. The student will be engaged in a complex, essentially intellectual process of searching for and identifying a set of ideas appropriate to an academic task of some kind. He will be looking for relations and patterns to fit to a pre-existing mental grid laid down to a certain extent by authority in the shape of teacher and critics. The question of enjoyment or the quality of reader/text interaction will rarely be given any priority although it may well be there. Books read outside the academic context are approached in a very different way. The quality of interaction is important, expressed on a scale of extreme boredom to passionate interest. Motivation is internal and expectations are different. The grid applied to the text is wider and more flexible. The time-factor is open-ended. In a very real sense the general reader engages in an ongoing relationship with a work which can last a lifetime of re-reading. Academic re-reading tends to terminate with the final examination.

It is, of course, slightly misleading to talk about two kinds of reading activity. Every act of reading constitutes a unique set of situational and personal circumstances. Nevertheless the features outlined above are broadly applicable for foregrounding the problems of reading and studying literature. It is a characteristic of academic situations to presuppose the existence and primary necessity of personal reading skills and to assume that the student is already equipped to make the intuitive responses and personal value judgements which constitute basic literary discourse, in spite of the fact that in many parts of the world students read little in their own language and even less in foreign languages. Even in those countries with a strong literary heritage, alternative forms of discourse are becoming increasingly dominant. Students are now more adept at 'reading' the audio-visual language of television and film and less adept in handling extended literary texts.

There is a need for developmental work on teaching the reading of literature as opposed to the study of literature, and it is in this that the interests and aims of both the language and literature teacher overlap. In saying this one is not denying the usefulness or importance of the examination of extrinsic features of text, but simply redressing an imbalance which has emphasized them at the expense of other aspects of the art of reading.

Much relevant material has appeared recently in the field of Applied Linguistics. Work on the analysis of texts has resulted in the flourishing sub-discipline of literary stylistics and some of the papers in this collection attempt to explore its relevance to overseas students, the pedagogical implications and the potential for language learning activities. Perhaps even more promising is the emergence of reader-centred approaches to comprehension in the fields of Psycholinguistics and Discourse Analysis which parallels developments in the literary school of the *nouvelle-critique*.

Work on discourse in relation to the study of reading comprehension has stressed the importance of the contextual features of utterances.[1] Comprehension is not just a matter of decorating the lexical and syntactic elements of the sentence. It is a more flexible and complex process involving the total context of the utterance, the rhetorical strategies of the text, and the attitudes, knowledge and expectations of the reader. The difficulty of a passage will not be the simple sum of its structural complexity but will depend on a unique set of linguistic and personal circumstances.

> . . . for the reader to 'comprehend' discourse means his being able to make sense of the discourse as a whole. I see no point in trying to distinguish between 'adequate'

comprehension (which is in no sense adequate) and 'total' comprehension (which will never be total). Comprehension must be a provisional construct by an individual, based partly on a language text, partly on the knowledge and skills he brings to the text. If this involves accepting 'different' comprehensions (which it does), then we will just have to be flexible about this.

(Urquhart, p.45)

In addition psycholinguistic theory has focused on the influence of motivational factors on perceived meaning in which the final result will depend on 'what the reader wishes to achieve' and 'his competence in utilizing the printed text in order to extract the meanings appropriate to his intentions'.[2]

One can compare this with literary critics of the structuralist school. In his survey[3] of their work on 'decoding' the text, Hawkes says:

Perhaps 'decode' is a misleading term here, for it suggests that there exists an ultimately 'uncoded' message. This is not the case, for as we have seen in the work of Whorf, Sapir and Lévi-Strauss, all our experience is 'coded' for us ultimately by our total way of life. A better term would be 'recode', by which is meant the activity of reducing or 'trimming' all experience to make it fit the categories we have ready for it.

Thus according to Scholes (*Structuralism in Literature: An Introduction*, Yale University Press, 1974, p.145) the job of the critic is 'readings that are more or less rich, strategies that are more or less appropriate'. Mick Short, in one of the papers in this volume, gives this reader-centred approach an intriguingly different twist by suggesting that a text might be defined as literature if it is read in a literary way.

Not all the contributors to this collection would take such a subjective attitude to meaning. Alex Rodger for example stresses the importance of language sensitivity based on a wider knowledge of language variety and an ability to recognize and analyse objectively how language is being used in a text. The effort here is to ascertain what the author is doing with the language in order to see what he meant. In this respect it is, albeit indirectly, an author-centred approach to meaning. But with its concern for 'communication awareness' it sees such analysis as an indispensable aid to the achievement of genuine reader/text interraction, and a personal response to the work.

All the authors, however, share a willingness to take a fresh look at what is involved in the reading and studying of literature and its language. It is hoped that such a collection of papers will demonstrate the intimate relationship between language and literature studies and generate thought and experimentation in syllabus design and teaching method which will be to the benefit of both language and literature teachers. The aim must be to bring back the element of enjoyment to the reading of literature with the recognition that it is not something to be ashamed of or avoided, but an indispensable part of the reading process in general.

Notes

1. A. H. Urquhart, 'Comprehension: the discourse analysis view: meaning in discourse', in *The Teaching of Comprehension*, ETIC. 1978, pp.25–47.
2. Keith Gardener, 'Reading Comprehension' in *The Teaching of Comprehension*, ETIC, 1978, p.71.
3. Terence Hawkes, *Structuralism & Semiotics*, Methuen, 1977, p.104.

THE DEVIANT LANGUAGE OF POETRY

H. G. WIDDOWSON

University of London Institute of Education

This paper was originally prepared as a public lecture at Wolfson College, Cambridge in February 1980 for a varied audience of linguists, literary scholars and language teachers. Its purpose was to bring these different interests to converge on matters of common concern by showing how certain central theoretical issues in linguistics can be interpreted to have a crucial bearing on an understanding of the nature of poetry, and so to point to the inter-relevance of literary and linguistic studies.

The paper does not address itself directly to questions of pedagogy. The appropriateness of its inclusion in this collection rests on the assumption that a principled methodology for the teaching of poetry must depend on a prior awareness of its essential character as a kind of discourse. The main implication for teaching is that since the uniqueness of poetry as a mode of meaning can only be recognized and appreciated against the background of conventional uses of language, then poems ought to be presented in association with instances of other kinds of discourse and attention directed to the differences between them.

'To circumscribe poetry by a definition', says Samuel Johnson in his *Lives of the Poets* 'will only shew the narrowness of the definer.' Nevertheless I intend to take that risk and try, concentrating on lyric poetry as the paradigm case. Such attempts have been made before of course and I simply follow the great tradition, or if you prefer it the common pursuit. '. . . words set in delightful proportion . . .' (Sydney), '. . . the very image of life expressed in its eternal truth . . .' (Shelley), '. . . the spontaneous overflow of powerful feelings . . .' (Wordsworth). And more recently Ezra Pound: 'Poetry is a composition of words set to music. Most other definitions of it are indefensible, or metaphysical.' Whether this applies to the definition I shall offer I must leave it to you to judge.

Whatever else literature may be, we will agree that its effects are achieved through the medium of language. And here we encounter our first difficulty. The term is ambiguous. On the one hand it may refer to the underlying system of common knowledge, *langue* and on the other to particular realization of this knowledge as instances of behaviour: *parole*. F. W. Bateson provides a recent reminder of this distinction:

'*Langue*, you will remember, is the speech system, the vocabulary, accidence and syntax that a speech group learns, adjusts and stores away in its individual memories for use when required . . . *Parole*, on the other hand, is the particular speech act . . .'

He then goes on to say:

'The literary artifact . . . is *parole*'

(Bateson 1961:74)
(quoted in Butler and Fowler 1971:Extract 285)

Since linguists from de Saussure onwards, have been essentially concerned with *langue*, (the argument runs) what they have to say is of limited relevance to the student of literature. For 'he (the student of literature) is concerned only with *la parole*, a series of individual communicative acts, individual applications of the code.' (Hough 1969:104)

It should be pointed out perhaps that nowadays the linguist's attention is not focused so fixedly on *langue* as it has been in the past. There is an increasing interest in aspects of *parole* and a concern to account for those 'particular speech acts' and the 'individual communicative acts' that Bateson and Hough refer to. The linguist can no longer be kept at bay by the observation that the literary artifact is *parole*. But *is* it *parole*? On closer investigation, the answer seems less than self-evident.

Consider, for example, how one would characterize the following expressions:

The door is strange to be unlocked.
Slept Rip Van Winkle twenty years.
He saw not the beautiful lady.
I to him turn with tears.
It sads me in my heart to leave you.
When will you your round me going end?
There looked a strange man through the window.
When will you under be my roof?

If these were produced by a foreigner, one would be disposed to say that he lacked command of the language, and that what he comes out with is 'not English'. So these would be characterized as instances of *parole* which are referable to some linguistic system other than that of English. Such a system would be an unstable interlanguage, a transitional *langue* of a kind, though dissociated from any established social domain of use. But what if these expressions were produced by native speakers of English competent in the standard language? One might counter the question by saying that they wouldn't be, unless the speaker in question were temporally incapacitated by some condition which induced mistakes in performance—affected by fatigue or drink or drugs, or crazed with care or crossed in hopeless love. Involuntary distortions, correctable by sober reflection. But then what is one to say about the following:

God with honour hang your head,
Groom and grace you, bride, your bed
With lissome scions, sweet scions,
Out of hallow'd bodies bred.

Each be other's comfort kind:
Deep, deeper than divined,
Divine charity, dear charity,
Fast you ever, fast bind.

Then let the march tread our ears:
I to him turn with tears
Who to wedlock, his wonder wedlock,
Deals triumph and immortal years.

(G. M. Hopkins: *At The Wedding March*)

One must suppose that the distortion is deliberately fashioned for an effect. One does not react by accusing Hopkins of incompetence and correcting his English. Now consider another of our examples:

When will you your round me going end?

But how do we react to precisely the same syntactic deviation in the following lines (Hopkins again):

When will you ever, Peace, wild wooddove, shy wings shut,
Your round me roaming end, and under be my boughs?
When, when, Peace, will you, Peace?

(G. M. Hopkins: *Peace*)

It will not now do to say: 'What he really means is:'

When will you ever . . . stop roaming round me and be under my boughs?

because this normalization does *not* mean the same as the original. Hopkins' syntactic arrangement is, we must suppose, a deliberate act of artistry designed to achieve a particular meaning.

By now you will be suspecting that all of the examples of deviant expressions I have provided are taken from poetry.

Slept Rip Van Winkle twenty years.   Longfellow?
The door is strange to be unlocked.   Dylan Thomas?

In fact all the others are attested instances of learner error and are taken from a compendium of such errors entitled *The Gooficon* (Burt and Kiparsky 1972).

We cannot then judge by appearances. An error is taken as evidence of deficient competence in the language and calls for correction: a deliberate literary deviation on the other hand is taken as evidence of more than common mastery — after all poetry is according to Coleridge the best words in the best order. Yet we cannot distinguish between them as far as their outer form is concerned. Only when we know their origin do we know whether to deplore or praise.

So it is that if a foreign learner ventures to use the language creatively, with deliberate intent — 'The march,' he might say, 'The march treads our ears.' — he is likely to be condemned for his innovation. That's not English. But then why does it suddenly become English when it appears in a poem by Hopkins? The *parole* of the learner is the projection of an interlanguage which represents a different kind of *langue* from that of standard English. Then it is surely the case that the *parole* of the poem is also the realization of a different kind of *langue*. The literary artefact, we might say in reply to Bateson, exists precisely because it is NOT *parole* in any straightforward sense. It is in a way. But again in another way, it is not, since it does violence to accepted rule.

It is in a way; in the sense that it is recognizably related to the system of a particular language: a poem, in English, no matter how curiously wrought, is not mistaken for one in French or Swahili or any other language. On the other hand, the language items are not simply projected as tokens of established linguistic types. Often, there are no types that they can be tokens of, as we have seen. This is not to say that deviation from the rules of the linguistic system is a necessary or a sufficient condition for poetic effect. But whether or not language items in the poem conform to type, they always contract relations with other items within the context and so create significant regularities over and above those required by the language system from which they derive. They are significant because they signify. The phonology of English, for example, requires no alliteration, assonance, rhyme or metric measure in message forms but these sound patterns are used in poems to fashion a design of sound which combines with syntactic and lexical arrangements to create a code for the occasion. And elements in that extempore code take on a particular meaning value accordingly.

Consider an example. The word RIVER. Its signification appears in the Shorter Oxford Dictionary as follows:

> RIVER. A copious stream of water flowing in a channel towards the sea, a lake, or another stream.

But when the word is worked into the language patterns of poems it takes on meaning as a feature of their design, just as familiar and commonplace objects become a part of the configuration of colour and form in a painting, and so acquire a particular significance.

> Never did sun so beautifully steep
> In his first splendour valley, rock or hill;
> Ne'er saw I, never felt a calm so deep!

The river glideth at his own sweet will:
Dear God! the very houses seem asleep;
And all that mighty heart is lying still.

(Wordsworth)

The river sweats
Oil and tar
With the turning tide
With the turning tide

(Eliot)

Five miles meandering with a mazy motion,
Through wood and dale the sacred river ran,
Then reached the caverns measureless to man,
And sank in tumult to a lifeless ocean . . .

(Coleridge)

From too much love of living,
From hope and fear set free,
We thank with brief thanksgiving
Whatever gods may be
That no life lives for ever;
That dead men rise up never;
That even the weariest river
Winds somewhere safe to sea.

(Swinburne)

In each case the word takes on a different value in the unique frame of reference created by the internal patterns of language with the poem.

But it is always the case, it might be objected, that words take on particular referential value when they are used in context, when they appear in *parole*, no matter how commonplace. So *river* might on different occasions refer to the Thames, the Amazon, the Cam; might be associated with bridge building, military manoeuvres, romantic assignations and so on. This of course is true. Words are variables which take on different values in context. But these values are established by the normal operation of syntax and so are explicit projections of the conventional code. There is an accretion of particular attributes but *the* river remains *a* river, a token of a type, always and only a copious stream of water. In poetry this is not so. Here there is no simple accretion but a fusion of distinct category types to create a new category for the nonce. The river is not only a copious stream, it is also the deep clam of nature, or grease and sweat, or a mysterious movement in dreams, or the weariness of life. And all this because the word fits into place in a unique pattern of language in the poem, a pattern of sound and lexical association and syntactic form created by arrangements which have no dependence on the conventional functioning of syntax. The river that glideth at his own sweet will, the river that sweats oil and tar, the sacred river five miles meandering with a mazy motion, the weariest river that winds somewhere safe to sea are not just different instances of the same thing, they are also quite different things because they appear in different contextual designs. These designs constitute a secondary code, as it were, independent of the primary code of the language system as such.

In conventional discourse, the form that the message takes other than that dictated by syntactic rule does not matter to its meaning. Paraphrase leaves it unaltered. But in poetry it does matter and when it is changed the meaning changes also. No paraphrase is possible. This is because one is translating from a contextually determined code which has no generative power outside the message form of the particular poem.

I am suggesting, then, that in a poem we have two co-existing systems locking into each other so that terms take on two values simultaneously. Sometimes these values may be consistent one with the other, sometimes they may create a conflict which has to be reconciled. Conflict occurs for example in the occurrences of *river* we have been considering: in the conventional code the word has the feature of inanimacy but in the code of the poem it is animate: the river glideth at his own sweet will, the river sweats, the weariest river. Contradictions impossible in the ordinary world are fused here and reconciled. So what we have is a double structure, of *parole* which is also *langue*, of *langue* which is also *parole*, neither one nor the other, and yet both. A paradox, an anomalous hybrid. No wonder Empson remarks that 'the machinations of ambiguity are among the very roots of poetry'. (Empson 1961:3)

My use of the expression 'double structure' to refer to this unique convergence of linguistic patterning in poetry is in a way an act of deliberate provocation. The term already has a well-established sense in linguistics. But the way in which this sense differs from what I intend by the term is, I think, of particular significance for the definition of poetic discourse. In linguistics, double structure refers to the fact that the units at the phonological level only function internally within the language system itself to form higher level units. Sounds have no direct executive function in language use. In consequence they are not themselves meaningful but only provide the means for forming units which are: words. Thus the substantial character of a word, the sounds of which it is composed, does not determine its reference or the sense relations it contracts with other words. The relationship of sound and meaning is of its nature arbitrary. We return to de Saussure. For him the arbitrary relationship was one of two 'primordial characteristics' of the linguistic sign, and represents one of the two basic principles of language. But in poetry this principle is not operative. As we have noted, sounds are fashioned into designs which *are* meaningful: the patterns of language are significant beyond their function of realizing the rules of the conventional code, and this is why there can be no transposing into a different message form by paraphrase without radical alternation of meaning. So it is that the double structure of poetry, the convergence of patterns, necessarily depends on the denial of double structure as a primordial characteristic of the linguistic sign. Poetry operates on a fundamentally different and contrary principle from that which informs conventional language use.

I said that de Saussure pointed out the arbitrary nature of the linguistic sign as one of two primordial characteristics or basic principles of language. The other one does not apply to poetry either. It is the *linear* nature of the signifier. The importance of this principle, says de Saussure, equals that of the first principle: 'the whole mechanism of language depends upon it'. (de Saussure 1966:70). But the whole mechanism of poetry depends in large part on the undermining of the principle. For poems are not simply linear. Their very appearance on the page, their rhyme scheme, their rhythmic shape are devices for overcoming the limitations of linearity determined by syntax so that we are presented with a series of pattern units, with each one finding its place in the overall arrangement. This is a consequence, of course, of the transfer of the principle of equivalence from the paradigmatic to the syntagmatic axis of language (see Jakobson 1960). Once this transfer is made and equivalent items are actually realized within the message form itself, then they will inevitably project a two-dimensional design which transcends linearity.

Not surprisingly, this curious mode of language use calls for an adjustment to our customary reading habits. We would normally reject the form of the message as waste product, once it had served its purposes of conveyance, so as to extract the conceptual gist. The reading of poems, however, requires a conservation of message forms by recurrent acts of focusing so that the forms are realized as parts of the design as a whole,

> where every word is at home
> Taking its place to support the others . . .
> The complete consort dancing together . . .
> (Eliot)

The words of a poem are arranged like notes in music or steps in a dance: they appear in a succession but create a depth in harmony and movement, as if the co-ordinates of spatial relations were transposed into temporal arrangement. One can now appreciate the force of Ezra Pound's definition of poetry as 'a composition of words set to music'.

The double structure of poetry denies the principle of arbitrariness and creates a two-dimensional mode of expression which transcends the principle of linearity. Poetry is a deviant kind of discourse which exploits the resources of conventional language in order to develop contradictory quasi-systems of its own, systems compounded of both *langue* and *parole* which derive from a disruption of normal linguistic principles. But to what purpose? What is the point of such topsy-turvy activity?

It follows from their very nature that these contradictory nonce systems are only valid for the occasion for which they were created. They generate no messages outside the poem. They are useless for any further purpose. Conventional kinds of discourse, conforming as they do to normal linguistic principles, fit into a continuity: they are located in ongoing social life which is serviced by the conventional code. When I speak or when I write I do so in response to some requirement and I anticipate some consequence: my discourse is located in a contextual continuum and it has to conform to rule so that it may mediate my involvement in ordinary social interaction. But poetry is not and cannot be part of a continuum in this way. It is essentially dislocated from context, set aside: it presupposes no previous or existing situation outside that created by itself, it anticipates no continuation. It exists apart, complete in itself, self-contained within its own pattern. And no matter how fully our minds may be *engaged* by the situation created by a poem we can never be *participants*: it exists in a different plane of being. Consider this example:

> She walks in beauty, like the night
> Of cloudless climes and starry skies,
> And all that's best of dark and bright
> Meet in her aspect and her eyes . . .
>
> (Byron)

Who e'er she be, we should note (thinking of Crashaw) this is an impossible she, for, contrary to standard rule, the definite personal pronoun here refers to no definite person. We do not know at the end of the poem who is being described. And since she appears in a poem it would not be proper to ask, as Byron would no doubt be the first to agree. And now, another lady:

> That's my last Duchess painted on the wall,
> Looking as if she were alive. I call
> That piece a wonder, now . . .
>
> (Browning)

It is indeed a wonder, since, though pointed out to us as if it were present before our eyes, the picture is not there. It only exists, for all its immediacy, within the confines of the poem, closed off from contact with the world. It belongs to a quite different dimension of reality fashioned within the poem itself. There is no recourse to, and no need of, any circumstantial evidence provided by context.

The peculiar convergent system of poetic expression functions to realize speech acts which cannot occur in normal discourse: an identification which has nothing to identify:

> That's my last Duchess painted on the wall

A summons to someone who has no existence:

> Come into the garden, Maud.
>
> (Tennyson)

Or, rather more lustily, from Ben Jonson:

> Come my Celia, let us prove
> While we may, the sports of love . . .

A poem, then, proclaims its independence of contexts which normally condition our understanding of discourse, and instead fashions its own convergent double structure to compensate for this severance of connection. As a result, it realizes speech acts which have no validity in ordinary language interaction. What Searle 1969 refers to as 'normal input-output conditions', essential requirements for communication, just do not obtain. How can one characterize remarks addressed to entities which are of their nature non-participant third person things: nightingales and cuckoos, the west wind and a Grecian urn, daffodils and the lesser celandine, quite apart from less evocative vocatives, such as this from Wordsworth:

Spade! with which Wilkinson hath tilled his lands.

And William McGonegall (poet and tragedian):

O Beautiful railway bridge of the silvery Tay.

And what are we to make of speech acts supposedly *performed* by such entities: we are addressed by a hawk roosting, a windmill, a corpse, a cloud, a brook:

I come from haunts of coot and hern

What kind of speech act is that? None that we know of, or can know of outside the imagined and dissociated context of the poem.

So there can be no commitment to truth or to the normal conditions of communication in poems because there is a deliberate distortion of the means for discharging such a commitment. Poetry, as Graham Hough has observed 'exists within a parenthesis, as it were, distinguishing it from actual discourse'. It is not like real language. And yet, as Hough goes on to point out:

Within the parenthesis all the effects that have
been observed outside it are still active
(Hough 1969:28)

The words carry with them their ordinary language meanings, together with the aura of association that surrounds them because of the contexts of their most common occurrence. And these effects are indeed still active. Cuckoo and celandine, wind and river retain their reference to familiar phenomena, and remain tokens of shared experience. But their occurrence in the designed message form of the poem make them mean something more, for they appear as part of an unfamiliar pattern, dissociated from the company they would normally keep, and so they take on a strangeness. They are familiar because of the presupposed context they carry with them from normal use and unfamiliar because of the actual context in which they find themselves.

This 'dissociation of sensibility' based on a dissociation of sense by displacement of context is, I think, what art in general seeks to achieve. A mass of twisted metal removed from its normal setting in the scrap yard and placed on a pedestal in a public square forces a reconsideration of stock responses. So does a can of Cambells' soup isolated from the Supermarket shelves and put in a frame, and fire-bricks set out symmetrically in the Tate Gallery.

But this shift from normal patterns of occurrence would in ordinary circumstances simply cause confusion. We cannot live in a world where categories are unclear, where contraries combine, where there is no security in an established order sustained by the conventional language. Dislocation, disorientation, derangement: that way madness lies. But the chaos is recast into a different form in the patterns of the poem. The rhyme, the metrical arrangement, the whole design re-assembles the dislocated elements into an alternative order held in momentary balance in the pattern of the poem itself. Poetry, like the god Siva, is both destroyer and creator simultaneously.

From the Swiss linguist Ferdinand de Saussure to the Indian god Siva: a tortuous route, you may think, and a tenuous connection. But it seems to me that we cannot understand the aesthetic effect of poetry without recognizing what kind of discourse it is, and the nature of its deviance from normal language. Poems, I have argued, represent unique language systems in which the regularities of *langue* and *parole* converge, systems which are linguistic paradoxes in that they are based on a denial of the primodial characteristics of arbitrariness and linearity and have no power to generate other messages. They express, therefore, what no other use of language is capable of expressing: a kind of converse reality, a different existential order in another dimension of experience, a fugitive paradox held for a moment outside ordinary time and place. And since no other use of language can convey this, it seems best to leave the last word to a poet:

> Only by the form, the pattern,
> Can words or music reach
> The stillness, as a Chinese jar still
> Moves perpetually in its stillness . . .
> Here the impossible union
> Of spheres of existence is actual,
> Here the past and future
> Are conquered, and reconciled . . .
>
> (T. S. Eliot: *Four Quartets*)

References

Burt, M. and Kiparsky, C. (1972) *The Gooficon*, Rowley, Mass: Newbury House.
Butler, C. and Fowler, A. (eds) (1971) *Topics in Criticism*, London: Longman.
De Saussure, F. (1966) *Course in General Linguistics*, trans. Basker, W. New York: McGraw-Hill.
Empson, W. (1961) *Seven Types of Ambiguity*, Harmondsworth: Penguin Books.
Hough, G. (1969) *Style and Stylistics*, London: Routledge & Kegan Paul.
Jakobson, R. (1960) 'Concluding statement, linguistics and poetics' in Sebeok 1960.
Searle, J. R. (1969) *Speech Acts*, Cambridge: Cambridge University Press.
Sebeok, T. A. (ed) (1960) *Style in Language*, Cambridge, Mass: MIT Press.

APPROACHES TO THE STUDY OF LITERATURE: A PRACTITIONER'S VIEW

H. L. B. MOODY

formerly of The British Council, Colombia

1. The Problem

Once again we are concerned with the redefinition — for the 1980's as it were — of the role and management of literature in the curricula of educational systems of various levels and in various situations. It seems that enthusiasts have been doing this for generations, even centuries, and no doubt the need for such defences has to be seen as reflecting some of the perennial antinomies of human life on this planet. At least it is good to see the British Council returning to this question, which is not unconcerned with what Britain has to offer in cultural exchange with the rest of the world.

The present writer does not pretend to be dealing with the issues involved at a philosophical level. However, he hopes that the experiences of a practitioner — also hopefully *un homme moyen sensuel* — who has browsed around to collect 'the best that has been thought and known' in our time, and reflected on his own teaching of literature, may be admitted as some kind of testimony in the present campaign.

For those who feel uncertain, in the present cross-currents of intellectual adventure and curriculum revolution, as to whether the teaching and study of literature should still be maintained, it may be helpful to consider the following 'facts':

1. Literature(s) exist(s). The corpus of available texts in almost every language and culture, and at a variety of different levels, is substantial, and continues to grow. (For the moment we beg the question of what we mean by 'literature'.)

2. Literature commands respect — also enthusiasm and devotion. The emphasis varies from one reader, and one community, to another, but broadly speaking literature is valued and calls forth considerable spontaneous creature effort from both its producers and consumers (who often include those who are most seriously engaged in the affairs of their times).

3. Literature as a form of human activity, in spite of the apathey of

17

philistines and the scorn of some rival academic disciplines, continues
to flourish. Reasons for its survival include:
— its undeniable capacity to produce pleasure and enjoyment
  (whatever the psychological or ethical bases of these reactions) to
  ordinary readers in many walks of life — and therefore its ability to
  provide a living (whether meagre or sumptuous) to its producers.
— its contributions to cultural identity, national pride and social aims
  in developing societies throughout the world (and which societies
  are *not* developing?)
— its value as a component in education (both formal and non-
  formal), the processes by which human individuals gain awareness
  of themselves and of their worlds and are assisted to construct
  their value systems.

4.   Educational establishments in many parts of the world abound in
      teachers and students who have very positive memories of the place of
      literature in their own formation and who are eager to offer it as a
      component in modern education, though at present they tend to be
      dismayed by the encroachments of other subjects and no longer feel
      quite so confident of what the teaching of literature involves (in itself a
      very healthy sign).

2. The Task

The task is to organize, possibly to up-date, our ideas and mobilize our
resources: to make clearer to ourselves (as teachers), to our devotees and to
our critics, what we want to offer, and to define the benefits which may be
expected. The campaign needs to be carried on at several levels:
— the intellectual/academic, to ensure that the study of literature is
  seen as a valid and respectable discipline, based on a real and
  accessible area of reality and employing methods as rigorous as
  those used in any other discipline. Possibly this level is better
  served than the others by such authorities as Henry Widdowson,
  Jonathan Culler, and the teams mobilized by Roger Fowler:
— the educational/administrative, to ensure that those who control
  educational systems, plan curricula, commission materials,
  organize public examinations, give adequate recognition to the
  place of literary studies, especially as these may need to be
  modified in the light of current thinking.
— The curricular/pedagogic, to ensure that both those who teach
  literature, and those who teach other subjects, have a steady view
  of the potential of literature in the total curriculum, which is
  neither exaggerated nor undermined. Particularly important is it to
  ensure that teachers understand how to present literature (which
  may involve more than conventional teaching) so that its potential
  can be fully realized.
— the information of public opinion, to ensure that pressures

exercised, on individuals and on systems, by such agencies as the media, education committees, and parents, are in conformity with what is being attempted by professionals.

It appears a matter of some delicacy to strike the right note in reasserting the importance of literary studies. Some claims in the past have been too arrogant; some, at the present time, are perhaps too apologetic. What is required is the calm, objective statement that a component of literary studies is no less fundamental in any curriculum than a component of history, social studies, mathematics, science, art, religion, physical education or anything else. In specialized forms of training, such as the teaching of foreign languages, the way is also open for a realistic reconsideration of the role of literature.

3. Literature

Discussion of this topic is always hampered by the semantic cloudiness of the term 'literature'. Some years ago the then Bishop of Woolwich[1] suggested that questions of religious faith would be much better thought about if the word 'God' were suspended from use for a generation or so. In the same way, we need to discuss the present issue without getting tangled up in the unconscious connotations (whether adulatory or hostile) which the term literature almost always carries with it. So, what are we talking about?

By 'literature' we refer to constructions, or artefacts, in language, which may be designed for any of the whole range of human communication needs, private or public, oral or written, for which language is used. Vast accumulations of verbal artefacts exist in all languages, of varying degrees of seriousness, and all, according to the extent to which they are disseminated, play a significant role in developing the identity, aims and commerce of their respective language communities. Conventional academic classifications of literary genres (Poetry, Drama, Prose: Tragedy, Comedy, Farce, etc.) are woefully insufficient to describe the great gamut of verbal artefacts which constitute the literature of any language. Some of these artefacts obviously have a more ephemeral existence; others are of more permanent significance in relation to their specific culture.

To broaden the basis of our claims for literature, it is advisable to reduce the conventional differentiation between the literary and the non-literary. As a general title we should perhaps set aside the rather tendentious 'The Teaching of Literature' and use instead the more open 'Literary Studies' and for the individual artefact we can probably do no better than use the word *text*, so that Literary Studies is concerned with the study of texts. A 'text' is a verbal artefact (more or less deliberately created), with no preconditions as to social or cultural status, which is available in tangible form for study, analysis and evaluation. In any language there is obviously a vast range of texts, from those which are very unusual to those which are outstandingly ordinary.

Admiration for a tremendous novelty such as *Finnegans Wake*, however, should not inhibit our willingness to take an interest in products of a different order, let us say a play by Harold Pinter, a poem from a South African Bantustan, a circular from the Board of Inland Revenue, or a piece of personal writing by a primary school child. This corresponds quite closely with suggestions made in recent years by Widdowson who contends that 'the basic problem in the teaching of literature is to develop in the student an awareness of the what/how of literary communication, and this can only be done by relating it to . . . normal uses of language.[2] A collection of practice material by the present writer, devoted to the same idea, was published some years ago.[3]

It is, of course, essential that any planned course of literary studies, defined in this sense, should include a balanced selection of texts, ranging from those that are successful and highly significant to those that are commonplace or even failures, but we should avoid the pretentiousness which assumes that something claimed to be a poem necessarily represents a higher order of creative achievement than, say, a letter. It is certainly desirable that every course should include a proportion of texts which tend towards the status of being 'notable', otherwise the student will lose the opportunity of experiencing the aspects of greatness in linguistic form which any course should provide. The basic condition is that each text is there (on the page) available for interpretation, analysis, classification and evaluation with as much rigour and accountability as a sample of anonymous white powder by a chemist, or a stained micro-organism on a glass slide by a pathologist.

The expression 'on the page' (however honourable its ancestry) pulls us up short. Are we at the present day to be concerned only with those verbal artefacts which can be represented in graphic symbols? If we consider the modes in which the majority of us nowadays experience a considerable proportion of the texts (both major and minor) which we encounter in day-to-day life, it seems logical to allow a distinct place for the oral/aural mode and the media (films, radio, television). This is an area which most formal academic courses in literature have not yet attempted to enter — despite the respectability of drama. There are obvious practical problems, especially in making such texts available for study, but they are by no means impossible of solution, as Davy and Crystal have shown.[4]

4. The Study of Literature

So far we have been talking about the 'material' of our study. At this point an important distinction must be introduced. It is not enough to insinuate the study of literature, or texts, into a curriculum. It is important to specify the nature and value of the study to which it is submitted. A play of Shakespeare (or other 'set book') may rightly be regarded as an outstanding text, whether of the particular culture of an age or for all time. Yet we all know what the study of such a text can be reduced to in response to the exigencies of a public examination system in a competitive society. Literary studies, it seems, have always been liable to dilution and travesty, sometimes with the full connivance of professional men of letters, and its history abounds with attempts to restore it to what it ought to be. It is important, incidentally, to heed Lionel Trilling's apt warning some years ago[5] that not all the adulteration comes from one source, and that the second environment of enlightened criticism also brings its distinct dangers.

One of the best statements of an ideal for literary studies comes from Alex Rodger:

> I take it as axiomatic that our task (as teachers of literature) is not to hand over predigested meanings, but to teach our students how to read and interpret for themselves . . . not to indoctrinate them with an academically hall-marked and guaranteed set of received opinions . . . but to be reasonably skilled and sensitive readers, able to feel and judge for themselves, with fidelity to the textual facts, in response to any work of literature they may choose to read.[6]

This is very useful so far as it goes, and it would be a great advance if all literary studies could match up to these axioms. Yet undoubtedly something more is also needed if we are to establish our calling as a respectable discipline, standing shoulder to shoulder and entering into full conversation with its fellows. The British tradition of literary studies, in contrast to those of continental Europe and the Americas, has long been suspicious of 'theory' (which perhaps means 'bad at thinking'), placing its faith aggressively in various forms of empiricism (practical criticism) which need no explanation among friends. We can no longer afford this self-indulgence, and must set forth our principles and procedures in terms which permit question, discussion, and verification. We need two things:

1. A Theory of Literature, brought up-to-date and assimilated to other intellectual movements of the day.

2. An Approach to the Text, derived from the theory and applicable by practitioners at various levels to suitable selections of texts for any pedagogic situation.

5. A Theory of Literature

My suggestion is that for a comprehensive theory we go back at least to I. A. Richards, collect all that is of value in Wellek and Warren, and bring these elements into a new synthesis with judicious help from de Saussure, the semiologists, the social anthropologists, the cyberneticists, or what can perhaps less alarmingly (to some people) be referred to as the exponents of communication theory. Richards, back in 1924,[7] faced with a 'chaos of critical theories', seized upon communication as the central idea in his attempts to justify the arts (including literary criticism). The development of information theory during recent years has considerably extended our appreciation of the importance and diverse nature of communications in the existence of civilized societies. In Bathesian terms,

> the whole human activity of working out, exchanging and preserving information should be seen as a unity which is composed of immanently organized but interrelated semiotic systems not one of which can function in isolation.[8]

From this view, which sees literature as only one strand (albeit a very important one) in a complex communications network, we gain further justification for emphasizing the relationship between the literary and the non-literary; also between the literature of the book, and the literature of the media.

Besides communication, Richards was also (somewhat uneasily) concerned with questions of 'value', and in this delicate area a synthesis between communications, literature and culture (but not Culture) provides a better criterion than the sensibilities of some Cultural élites. Value will be related with the mainsprings of motivation and action in a specific cultural context.

The theory can be spelt out more explicitly as follows:

1. Human welfare depends on the full development 'on all sides of our humanity' of the individual, but the individual can only realize himself in society, and it is essential for him (or her) to belong to and participate in the life of a community. In fact he/she will usually participate in a variety of interlinked communities (family, age group, town, profession, party, nation, etc.)

2. A community is important for the individual, not only as providing the basics — food, shelter, help when needed — but also as maintaining a culture, a coherent, reasonable, effective way of life, complete with customs, institutions, ideology, entertainments, rituals, and value systems. Cultures in this anthropological context can, of course, vary considerably in sophistication, refinement, and strength.

3. Communications are essential for the maintenance of a culture. They occur in various forms: the physical, the linguistic, the social, the artistic: footpaths, bridges, roads, telephones, radio programmes; leaflets, magazines, books, laws; conversations, meetings, religious services, civic ceremonies; music, dancing, costume, painting and sculpture, architecture, sports, TV. All these (the list is not exhaustive) are well described as 'amplifiers of culture'.

    Communities sometimes fail from disease, starvation, military conquest, inadequate economic resources: more often they fail, even if less dramatically, from lack of adequate communications.

4. Literature, the spoken word and the written word, comes into the

processes of cultural amplification at many levels, in both more and less institutionalized ways. The various levels are often closely interconnected, e.g. the novel with commercial advertisement, poetry with religious observances, drama with play, laws with political propaganda, etc.

5. The study of literature, verbal artefacts, is an essential element in our understanding and control of the communities in which we live. There is the question of efficiency, of saying what we really want to say, 'of keeping the tools of language clean'. There is also the problem of discrimination: in view of the multitude of verbal artefacts to which we are continuously submitted, of distinguishing those which are valid and worthwhile from those which are not.

6. An Approach to Literature

The value of a theory is to ensure that we know what we are doing at any particular point, and can defend it. The importance of an Approach (or method) is to provide a framework, or sequence of operations to be used when we come to actualities, in this case to the study of particular texts. In the past, it has often been here that the teaching of literature has faltered and students have been led busily but aimlessly through forests of 'inspired literary gossip', or cajoled into rigid and doctrinaire interpretation — ethical, political, aesthetic or linguistic.

The approach now recommended recognizes that every text is likely to be a complex entity, and capable of analysis and commentary from a variety of different points of view. We take from Wellek and Warren,[9] whose clear-minded exposition is well worth rereading from time to time, the distinction between the Extrinsic and the Intrinsic.

7. The Extrinsic

In various ways any text can be seen as determined by external factors which account for its existence or its special features. The principal ones would be:

1. *The biographical.* Every text has been produced (let us assume) by a particular writer, living at a particular time in a particular place, and at a particular point in his own career, for particular needs. It is certainly relevant at a certain stage to know these facts and to be aware of how they influence the content and form of a particular text. [For traditional or folk literature some modification of this assertion is necessary.]

2. *The historical.* Every text has been created at a particular point in historical time, and may bear the evidence of historical processes, whether economic, social, political, or ideological. (A special type of

influence may be that of literary history.) If we take the view that history continues right up to the moment of a text's creation, this approach can be taken also to include the sociological, in which the text is seen to reflect various aspects of the social context in which it has been produced.

3.   *The aesthetic.* By this we refer to the ways in which a particular text can be seen to reflect various theoretical or practical movements, related to the processes of artistic creation, general problems of form, structure, uses of language, prosody, genres, etc.

4.   *The philosophical.* At this level, we recognize that texts can be seen to illustrate topics typically belonging to other disciplines such as, for example, ethics, metaphysics, psychology, theology, perhaps even science or mathematics.

These extrinsic approaches reflect the interests of various specialists who may be drawn to literature to further, or illustrate, their own enquiries. Incidentally, they also reflect the different kinds of background knowledge which the well-trained reader will bring to the interpretation of texts. [There is here a link with current psycholinguistic explanations of 'reading comprehension', in which an important factor is the reader's ability to relate information discovered in a text to information already possessed from other sources.]

8.   The Intrinsic

Of course no text can be made use of in any way until it has been read and assimilated, and the intrinsic approach consists of all the processes which are carried out, more or less consciously, in their various sequences and at their various levels, in the course of a complete reading. Broadly, the main levels are:

1.   *The grammatical.* The organization of units of expression both within the sentence, and between sentences.

2.   *The lexical.* This includes not only the denotations and connotations of words, and lexical groups, but also questions of register, style, figurative language, etc.

3.   *The structural.* Here we think not of sentence structure, but of the 'analysis of discourse' the organization of complete texts of whatever kind, whether expository, narrative, argumentative or symbolic. This will include effects of patterning, rhythm, etc.

4.   *The cultural.* Here, at the semantic level, we are concerned with the

content, the 'message', what is presented, or stated, or implied, and its value in relation to the cultural context.

All these components, in both the extrinsic and the intrinsic approaches, can be stated quite simply. In their recognition in particular texts, of course, the investigation can become highly complex. If the question is asked which must be attempted first, the extrinsic or the intrinsic, the answer is that here we are merely concerned to describe the elements of the two approaches theoretically, and that in practice the process of reading is likely to move backwards and forwards between the two elements, as the mind of the reader takes in new information, constructs temporary schemata, verifies or rejects them, forms further predictions of what is still to come, and begins the process of evaluation. We could say that the extrinsic approach is concerned with what the reader *brings* to the interpretation of a text, the intrinsic approach extricates the fresh information he discovers in it. The extrinsic approach involves what is implicit in a text, the intrinsic with what is made explicit. Not all texts which may be encountered necessarily exhibit all the potential components.

Another way of illustrating the difference between the Extrinsic and the Intrinsic is by reference to the great curriculum innovation (long before Nuffield science) described, now fifty years ago, by I. A. Richards in *Practical Criticism*.[10] Richards, suspecting that much traditional academic information is likely to inhibit the capacity to read and respond naturally to a text, required his students to evaluate pieces of verse (no prose at that time) presented entirely anonymously, with no extrinsic information about authorship, date, title, topiç, academic standing, etc. Without commenting further on this experiment and Richards' analysis of the results, we can say that readers in such a controlled situation were obviously entirely dependent on an intrinsic approach, utilizing only information contained within the 'protocols' themselves.

If a visual model of a text could be considered helpful. It might be constructed on the analogy of a cell, in which the inner nucleus or core (the intrinsic) is surrounded by a more diffuse outer envelope (the extrinsic) which permits the cell to enter into more extended relationships (corresponding to a culture), see page 26.

No doubt better models could be proposed and constructed. The validity of the model, and the approach it is based on, of course, have to be tested in use for the interpretation of a series of texts.

9. The Approach Illustrated

To suggest how our approach can be carried out in practice, we offer four demonstrations: within the limits of a paper such as this, the texts are quite

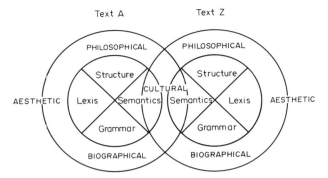

short, and the various types of information extracted or presented are given in fairly concise form; it is supposed that the method is capable of as much expansion as necessary.

TEXT 1

Nature, and Nature's Laws, lay hid in night:
God said *Let Newton be*! and all was light.

INTRINSIC

1. **Grammar.** Two short statements, each of ten syllables. The first with double subject, Nature and its equal counterpart, Nature's Laws; both are said to have been 'dark'. The colon at end of the first line indicates a time interval: *at last* God said something, 'and' — which signifies 'after that' or 'as a result of that' — the situation changed.
2. **Lexis.** Nature — in which sense? The romantic? Nature as something giving, or obeying Laws! Therefore not romantic. Nature 'lay hid in *night*', i.e. in darkness, obscurity, ignorance, 'lay' suggests passivity. Then 'Newton' came into the picture, after which night turned to 'light' — signifying clarity, understanding, enlightenment (conventional symbolism). Who was Newton? Sir Isaac, apple,

EXTRINSIC

1. **Biographical.** Alexander Pope (1688–1744)'s epitaph for Newton (1642–1727) in Westminster Abbey, where VIP's were often buried, (e.g. Poet's Corner). Did Pope know Newton personally? (Did Newton know Pope?) What kind of social, intellectual contacts did they have? Who asked Pope to write this? Was it actually used? Is it still there?
2. **Historical.** Intellectual developments in seventeenth century, from medieval scholasticism, authoritarianism to the rational, empirical tradition (Bacon, Descartes, etc.). Founding of Royal Society, 1662. Newton's career and publications, *Principia Mathematica* (1687), in Latin (?). His standing in English Society. Augustans.
3. **Aesthetic.** Interest of Augustans

gravity, laws of motion, etc. Familiar allusion (almost parody) to Genesis 1:3 — the arrival of Newton as important as God's creation of Light! Perhaps the creation of Newton a part of God's plan of creation and relevation.

3. **Structure.** Rhythmic balance between the two lines, giving maximum weight to the important antithesis being the rhyme words, 'night' and 'light'. Whole meaning kept in suspense until final word 'light', which unlocks the allusion to Genesis. The balance between two lines also emphasizes contrast between ideas of 'before' (ignorance) and 'after' (enlightenment).

4. **Culture.** This is a way of conveying the critical importance of Newton's 'discoveries' in man's evolving understanding of the universe. The economy of words, and neat balance, give it great force, and the biblical allusion associates it with weighty issues. A powerful statement about an important fact of human history.

in myth and epic (e.g. *Paradise Lost*): exploring also possibilities of mock-epic (e.g. *The Dunciad*) Augustan adoption of the 'heric conflet' symbolizing their search for 'balance?' There taste for 'wit' (unexpected ways of saying things). Pope, a satirist, notorious for his attacks on his literary enemies: but he also knew how to praise.

4. **Philosophical.** Various concepts of Nature, in Western christian philosophy — and other systems. The Augustans' perception of an ordered, rational Universe, giving evidence of a rational creator. Natural religion (deism). Theories of revelation — once and for all (the fundamentalists)? or gradual and evolutionary? God reveals himself to man through creation (which still goes on — a continuous process), which includes selected and gifted prophets, individuals (see Newton) who step by step reveal 'the secrets of the universe'. Modern attitudes towards Newtonian physics, etc.

TEXT 2

Young lady, you are:
A mirror that must not go out in the sun
A child that must not be touched by dew
One that is dressed up in hair
A lamp with which people find their way
Moon that shines bright
An eagle feather worn by a husband
A straight line drawn by God

INTRINSIC

1. **Grammar.** Surprisingly simple — address to 'young lady' in form

EXTRINSIC

1. **Biographical.** From a collection of *Igbo Traditional Verse*, first

of series of seven assertions, all complements of 'are'.

2. **Lexis.** A few problems in recognizing full connotations of some items, probably because of special cultural apprehensions e.g. of 'mirror' — why should it not go out in the sun? Clearly she must be protected (e.g. from 'dew', admired, and respected. Obviously hair-style is important. 'Lamp' leads to 'moon'. The 'eagle feather' some token of special status, so she is the pride of her husband. Curiously, 'straight line' (uncommon, perfect, up-right) has Euclidean echoes. Indications are that this comes from a non-European culture and possibly therefore translated from another language.

3. **Structure.** A series of attributes of female charm, in increasing order of power, leading to a climax which is powerful enough to leave nothing more to be said.

4. **Culture.** This is a 'poem' designed to praise a young lady — ? poem of flattery. In this case her charm is related to youth and femininity: no special reference to character, intellect, skills, personality, achievement. Probably a culture in which individual qualities, especially of women, are not important, but beautiful females regarded, if not as 'sex-objects', at least as status symbols. However, the poem carries some force of personal feeling.

published in West Africa, 1971, and soon after in London. This is a folk poem, in which individual authorship is not recorded. Could have been written by a professional praise-singer, or by a lucky husband. Such poems are being collected nowadays in the process of retrieving and exhibiting the achievements of primitive culture.

2. **Historical.** Spread of Western culture, during last 150 years, among many colonized peoples (Africa, Asia, America). Contempt for other culture a prerequisite of colonization. The processes leading to political independence: acceptance, exploration, resentment, agitation, self-government: current need to assert cultural identity, by collecting evidence of the value and coherence of the traditional culture.

3. **Aesthetic.** The power and appeal of the 'primitive', in all the arts. Link between primitive and child art. But is it so simple? Much folk art bears analysis by the techniques originally developed for the appreciation of 'metropolitan' culture (e.g. Ruth Finnegan.)[11] In this poem some of the perceptions show a sophisticated 'wit'.

4. **Philosophical.** Such poems carry a characteristic value system, even if somewhat less articulated than a work from a more diversified culture. Need to think carefully about the Primitive (e.g. Lévi-Strauss' *La Pensée Sauvage*), which may have virtues greater than supposed during hey-day of colonization, — especially coherence, stability, adaptation to environment, etc.

TEXT 3

And religion, the greatest and most important of the efforts by which the human race has manifested its impulse to perfect itself, — religion, that voice of the deepest human experience, — does not only enjoin and sanction the aim which is the great aim of culture, the aim of setting ourselves to ascertain what perfection is and to make it prevail; but also, in determining generally in what human perfection consists, religion comes to a conclusion identical with that which culture, — culture seeking the determination of this question through *all* the voices of human experience which have been heard upon it, of art, science, poetry, philosophy, history, as well as of religion, in order to give a greater fullness and certainty to its solution, — likewise reaches, Religion says: *The kingdom of God is within you* and culture, in like manner, places human perfection in an internal condition, in the growth and predominance of our humanity proper, as distinguished from our animality . . .

INTRINSIC	EXTRINSIC
1. **Grammar.** Begins with 'and', continuing previous exposition: about 'religion', what does it actually say? — complex syntax, multiplication of appositions, repetitions, and parenthesis. Is it that:	1. **Biographical.** From Chapter 1 ('Sweetness and Light') of Matthew Arnold's *Culture and Anarchy: An Essay in Political and Social Criticism* (1869). Matthew, son of Thomas Arnold, famous headmaster of Rugby, responsible for uplifting the 'moral tone' of British public school education. Poet, critic (much followed by some twentieth-century critics), and early H M Inspector of Schools, much aware of social problems of the less privileged in prosperous Victorian Britain.

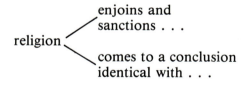

the same aims as culture?

Curious hanging clause ending with 'likewise reaches'. Interesting problem to diagram the first sentence.	2. **Historical.** Britain in 1869 a leading and prosperous industrial nation, full of John Bull-type confidence, associated with religious fervour (often of non-conformist type), a staunch individualism, and general doctrines of self-help, free-trade, laissez-faire, etc. Arnold a Liberal, but 'tempered by experience', eager to arrest the 'philistinism' of the middle class

S   V   O

religion   aims of culture

Is this involved syntax justified?

2. **Lexis.** Exposition centres round two prominent words, 'religion' and 'culture'. Writer appears to be using these terms in his own special sense, which he proceeds to define by the appositional statements. Is the passage overloaded with duplication? No, distinctions made by paired words, such as *is/prevail, enjoin/sanction, humanity/ animality, determining/determination*, are important! In spite of the theoretical approach, the writer still attempts a personal note, you/our.

3. **Structure.** Although at first difficult to follow, the sentence structure *is* logical, and organized so as to bring rhetorical emphasis on to principal concept. The involved syntax(?) expresses writer's sense of commitment to his argument, and perhaps calls forth the attention of the reader.

4. **Culture.** The writer seeks to show that 'religion' and 'culture' (defined in his sense) have common aims. Difficult to evaluate his exposition without fuller knowledge from context; however he emphasizes the complex and comprehensive nature of both, which seems to suggest an attack on dogmatism and exclusiveness (see C. P. Snow's *Two Cultures*).

and the 'barbarism' of the working class; campaigned for great intelligence and humanity ('sweetness and light') in national affairs. His belief in the importance of 'the state' to ensure the prevalence of 'the best that has been thought and known' establishes him as a forerunner of the Fabian-socialist movement, and the Welfare State, etc.

3. **Aesthetic.** One of the masters of nineteenth-century prose with an eloquence and fervour derived from 'preaching'. Also a very allusive writer, tending towards the slogan and catch-phrase. His prose related to his lyrical-moralistic poetry.

4. **Philosophical.** Before the days of social anthropology, Arnold anticipates the idea of culture as all-incisive — an important milestone in the history of the word 'culture'. His religious ideas, though unorthodox at the time, contribute to the humanistic type of Christianity more typical of the twentieth century, with less emphasis on dogmatism and more on social action.

TEXT 4

The home of an ordinary, peaceable man was entered one day by a large and violent person, a person of great power and authority, who asked the man: 'Do you agree to serve me?' Without saying a word the man prepared food and drink for this person, and gave him the best room in the house and the best bed to sleep on. Washing and mending his clothes, cooking his meals, cleaning up after him, the man of the house served the intruder assiduously and without a word of complaint for seven years. At the end of this time the person of great power and authority had grown so fat, as fat even as the famous King of Egypt, and so unhealthy from lack of exercise that he died. The man wrapped the body in old sacking and threw it on a rubbish tip. Then he returned home, and burnt the bedding, washed the bedstead down with disinfectant, whitewashed the walls, scrubbed the floor-boards, and answered: 'No'.

INTRINSIC

1. **Grammar.** Logical, lucid, arrangement, yet carefully controlled: note passive, in the home 'was entered' (suggesting passivity). No opening courtesies, no preamble to the question 'Do you agree to serve me?'. No verbal response, yet the man proceeded to 'serve' and offer everything of his best. The intruder became 'fat' and eventually died. *Then* only comes the answer 'No'—rather curious, for the man did 'serve', even if he did not 'agree to'.

2. **Lexis.** Conventional phrases such as 'one day', 'for seven years' put this in the category of fable. Words chosen emphasize the submissive nature of 'the man', and the arrogance of the intruder, who accepts everything without appreciation or thanks. A significant contrast is developed between the 'grandeur' of the fat man (obscure allusion to the famous King of Egypt), and the unceremonious treatment he

EXTRINSIC

1. **Biographical.** This anecdote, quoted by D. J. Enright in *Memoirs of a Mendicant Professor*[12] described as 'after Brecht'. Brecht, founder of the important German dramatic group, Berliner Ensemble, introduced some important new ideas and techniques into stage drama ('epic drama', 'alienation effect', etc.) Most importantly he used drama to convey radical political messages. [Enright a writer with experience of Third World countries, and also sceptical of orthodox 'power' figures.]

2. **Historical.** As modern history has proceeded, liberal movements for emancipation, welfare, indepedence have spread around the world. At the same time (as predicted by Marxist philosophy) they have been met in many places by ruthless totalitarian régimes, which have unscrupulously repressed the interest of the small man.

received after his death (reminiscent of the end of many tyrants Macbeth, Hitler), wrapped in 'sacking', and thrown out as 'rubbish'. Following his disposal, the man proceeds to purify his house intensively. The blunt nature of his eventual answer 'No' matches the ungracious question asked by the intruder on taking over.

3. **Structure.** Apparently a simple story yet carefully balanced, with strong element of paradox. Curiosity is aroused when the man does not answer the question 'Do you agree . . .?' yet proceeds 'to serve'. His initial acts of service in past tense; then as they become continuous, a change to present participles, and they are gathered up in the words 'assiduously' and 'for seven years'. The next sentence blows up the effect of the intruder's fatness, to increase surprise when 'he died'. Interest to see what follows. The intruder is disposed of without ceremony. The actions of the man in cleansing his home more or less reflect, or undo his actions of service. His answer 'No', the final word, causes us to review the whole story, and see a different significance in the man's submissiveness; also it reflects ironically on the intruder's 'greatness'.

4. **Culture.** The simple enigmatic tale demands interpretation. The intruder represents — ? power, absolute power, tyranny, capitalism, colonization? The 'man', the ordinary man, is born to suffer, to endure, to wait. He

Collectivization, computerization, big business and automation, etc., all threaten the interests of the ordinary human being, and twentieth-century art and literature have tried to defend the 'human rights' of the individual. Brecht's achievements have been respected, not only behind the Iron Curtain, but throughout the world, and his influence on the theatre has been considerable.

3. **Aesthetic.** As part of his attack on false values, Brecht aimed to undermine the corrupt tastes of the bourgeois, their love of fantasy worlds, etc. His art is therefore sparse, dry, caustic, and the economic nature of this anecdote, which yet contains a consummate art, is very typical.

4. **Philosophical.** A key issue of our century has been the relation between the individual and the state (or other powerful organizations); often this becomes the conflict between the oppressed and the oppressor, the colonial people and the colonizing master race. There are various revolutionary approaches to this type of situation: open rebellion, defiance, protest; underground resistance, subversion, guerilla warfare: on the other hand, submission, whether weak or strong. (Fanon has the interesting concept of the 'Culture of Silence'). Some hope that all forms of excesses contain the seeds of their own disintegration, and acceptance is the best way of ensuring their defeat.

does not give his agreement to serve the tyrant, because he knows he has no alternative. Yet literally he has the last word. 'The meek shall inherit the earth': the tyrant is doomed by his own excesses.

10. Pedagogies

What we have so far attempted is to illustrate the model of a (literary) text which we have in mind as a basis for effective study. The question now has to be asked — that is the relevance of this model for actual teaching and study situations? What in fact is the recommended approach?

The characteristic of a teaching situation is that the teacher (hopefully) knows all, or at least a good deal, about the subject, topic, or text to which the learner is (for whatever reasons) to be introduced; the student, to begin with, knows nothing, or rather he does not know if he knows anything of relevance. How is the transfer of knowledge to the student to be effected? There are two extremes: on the one hand the teacher proceeds to 'tell' and to demonstrate to the learner all that he is intended to 'know'; on the other, he can leave the learner to his own devices, and say 'I'm leaving it to you to find out whatever is worth knowing about this.' On most occasions, a method midway between the extremes is preferable, and it is in devising this that the skill of the teacher is utilized. Firstly, the teacher needs to give whatever basic information is needed to help the student begin to study a new text whether as an inducement/incentive to begin on the right lines, or to avoid flagrant misreading. Secondly, he can devise a sequence of questions, or other activities, to help the student find his way through the various levels of significance which the text contains. It is in order to do this effectively that the teacher himself needs a comprehensive and correctly ordered appreciation of the text. Of course as students become more experienced and confident, they can be given a greater share of responsibility for organizing their study.

11. An Example

To illustrate a teaching procedure developed from the analysis of a text derived from a Theory of Literature, let us go back to Text No. 4, the Anecdote 'after Brecht'. We suggest five stages:

   1. Preliminaries
   2. Study procedure I } *Intrinsic*
   3. Study procedure II }
   4. More information
   5. Wider interests — Extrinsic

(Of course, students should not usually be bothered with distinctions of Intrinsic and Extrinsic. To them the study sequence should seem a spontaneous development of natural interests.)

We assume the text is being presented to middle secondary mother-tongue speakers, or first year university in an EFL situation.

Stage 1. *Preliminaries.* Here is a curious little story. It seems very simple, but it contains several unexpected features, which set you thinking. You will have to think out the story's real 'meaning', for it is certainly not stated openly.

Stage 2. *Answer these questions* (work may be done either individually or in groups, and answers presented in oral or written form):
1. Contrast the two characters in this story.
2. What is unusual about the visitor's first question?
3. List the services performed by the host for his guest. What do they imply?
4. What kind of communications seem to have occurred between the host and the guest during the seven years?
5. Account for the visitor's end.
6. What is significant about the way the body was disposed of?
7. List the activities of the man after returning to his home. What do they indicate?
8. Why did the man not answer the visitor's question sooner?

Stage 3. *Answer as many of these questions as you can* (work individually):
9. Like all fables, this story means something more than is openly stated. What in your opinion is the moral of the story?
10. What features account for the appeal of the story?
11. Discuss the extent to which each of the following words fits the story (or could be used as its title), and arrange them in order of suitability:

cowardice	arrogance
gluttony	cleanliness
prudence	delay
justice	patience.

12. Imagine the man, some time after the events of the story, talking to his son about political questions of the day. What would he be likely to say?
13. What features of the story, as actually set out, indicate that it is a fable?

Stage 4. *More information.*
'In fact, all we know about this story is that it is attributed to Bertolt Brecht (1898–1956), the famous German dramatist, founder of the acting company known as the Berliner Ensemble,

and author of such plays as *Mother Courage, The Caucasian Chalk Circle*'.

Stage 5.   14. *Carry out some library research on Brecht and report on the following*:
a. his political interests
b. his principal dramatic 'innovations'
c. his influence on British drama during the last 20 years.
15. How does the story seem typical of its author?
16. Compare the story with other representations of a similar nature in any medium. Some comparisons, for example, would be possible with:
a. Shelley's Sonnet *Ozymandias*
b. Franz Fanon's *The Wretched of the Earth* (Grove, 1965)
c. James Thurber's *Fable for Our Times*, 'The Glass in the Field' (in *Thurber Carnival* 1975).
d. Shakespeare's *Macbeth*
e. Picasso's *Guernica* (picture)

Comments on this suggested teaching sequence will be welcome.

Conclusion

In this paper we have attempted some justification for the continuation and development of literary studies, with suggestions about the way texts can be selected, analysed, presented, and studied. There is much more that might be said, and probably a good deal in this paper which needs amplification, defence, or correction. Two points which may be stressed, in conclusion:

1. The basic skill to be developed by the study of literature is the skill of reading (which is in fact, a set of diverse skills), and this if correctly managed is of relevance and value to all educated members of a free society.

2. Assuming that an appropriate selection of texts is made, students will delight in exercising and developing the reading skills, and we shall move nearer to the ideal, as recently formulated by Joshua Fishman[13] of our students 'knowing, using, and liking English'.

References

1. J. A. T. Robinson, *Honest to God*, SCM Press, 1963.
2. H. G. Widdowson, *Stylistics and the Teaching of Literature*, Longman, 1975, p. 70.
3. H. L. B. Moody, *Varieties of English*, Longman, 1970 (esp. Part II).
4. D. Davy and D. Crystal, *Investigating English Style*, Longman, 1969.
5. Lionel Trilling, *Beyond Culture*, Secker & Warburg, 1966. Chapter 8, 'The Two Environments: Reflections on the Study of English'.
6. Alex Rodger, 'Linguistics and the Teaching of Literature' in H. Fraser and W. R.

O'Donnell, *Applied Linguistics and the Teaching of English*, Longman, 1969, p.89.
7. I. A. Richards, *Principles of Literary Criticism*, Routledge & Kegan Paul, 1926.
8. R. Barthes, *Elements of Semiology* (translated from the French), Jonathan Cape, 1967.
9. R. Wellek and A. Warren, *Theory of Literature*, Penguin Books, 1963.
10. I. A. Richards, *Practical Criticism*, Routledge & Kegan Paul, 1929.
11. Ruth Finnegan, *Oral Literature in Africa*, Clarendon Press, 1970.
12. D. J. Enright, *Memoirs of a Mendicant Professor*, Chatto & Windus, 1969.
13. Joshua A. Fishman, 'Knowing, Using and Liking English as an Additional Language,' in *TESOL Quarterly*, Vol.II, No.2, June 1977.

LANGUAGE FOR LITERATURE

ALEX RODGER

University of Edinburgh

Introduction

This paper is about the linguistic needs of those who study and teach English literature in countries where English has the status of a second language, (ESL) and not that of a foreign one (EFL). Much of what I have to say is certainly relevant to the teaching of *any* literature which is not in the student's mother tongue and indeed all of it is of greater importance to the teaching of 'Eng. Lit.' in the United Kingdom than many home-based teachers seem prepared to admit. Nevertheless what has been called 'the Lang.-Lit. problem' in English studies at large[1] takes on a rather special character in ESL contexts where degree courses in English literature are conducted in the universities, and for that reason I address what follows primarily to those responsible for the design and teaching of such courses.

I have two related purposes here. The first is to provoke among ESL teachers a serious and radical reconsideration of the educational aims of English literature courses and of the methods used to attain those aims. The second is to suggest a methodological mini-model in the form of a step-by-step exploration of a very short 'poem by a major modern poet. This is presented from a pedagogical point of view in order to indicate how a teacher might handle this poem in the classroom as an exercise in which students are led, collectively and cumulatively, to discover for themselves what the poem is about and what its significance is likely to be, instead of being told these things in a lecture.

Part I of the paper is therefore theoretical in the sense that it is a logical consideration of the relationships between ends and means in ESL literary education, between the notional aims of teaching English Literature and the actual methods used to achieve them. The issues involved are far less simple than many teachers and student seem to be aware. Only the sketchiest account of them can be offered in a paper of this length, so readers are strongly urged to turn to the works most frequently cited in the notes, especially those of Leech[2] and Widdowson,[3] for a fuller rationale of the whole subject. My arguments are not, however, theoretical in the sense of being merely speculative and unrelated to practical experience, for my strictures upon much that passes for the teaching of English literature in many countries where English is an official second language are based upon a fairly wide range of first-hand acquaintance with these matters. I hope that the many good friends I have made among teachers and students overseas will accept these criticisms in the spirit in which I offer them, which is one of concern, counsel and, above all, cordial goodwill.

Part II, a suggested interpretation of Ezra Pound's well-known *In a Station of the Métro*, may strike some of my readers as absurdly long and over-technical in relation to the miniscule proportions of the poem itself. I can only plead that the complex business of making conscious and explicit to ourselves the reasons for our reactions to any literary work, however small, is not at all conducive either to brevity or to the stylistic elegancies of *belles-lettrism*, particularly when the writer has to explain the interpretative tools he is using as well as recommend how they might best be employed in the classroom. As for my own reading of the poem, I offer it not as *the* interpretation of this poem but as one which is as consistent as I can make it with the linguistic facts of the text, seen against the background of what we know about the normal workings of the English language. Its shortcomings are my own and not those of the method I advocate. A better stylistician would have done a better job.

PART I: Teaching Literary Skills—Problems and Principles

My title, *Language for Literature* is deliberately ambiguous because I want it to cover a number of different senses of the word 'language', which are all closely interconnected and of crucial importance to the effective teaching of literature. These notions of language relate to a number of basic principles which cannot be expounded fully here but can only be rather dogmatically summarized as follows.

1.   Literature as 'Foregrounded Discourse'

In any national language-community whatsoever, imaginative or creative writings of the kind instantly recognized and evaluated as literature constitute a special domain of linguistic communication. This differs markedly from the domain of non-literary communication but is neverthe-less dependent on it. Non-literary communication involves the use of conventionally appropriate kinds of language to convey practical everyday messages which are socially necessary and immediately useful. Literary messages such as poems, plays and novels make use of the same basic language-system (i.e. the grammar, the vocabulary, and the rules for combining these into meaningful utterances) as that used in the different kinds of non-literary discourse. But because literary messages differ from non-literary ones in function, i.e. in their communicative purposes, creative writers have to signal the fact of the literariness of their messages by inventing special conventions of poetic, novelistic and dramatic communication which would not work in ordinary practical discourse, and by using the language system itself in ways which are unorthodox, thought-provoking and striking. The result is that creative writers produce linguistic messages which, by their very nature, stand out prominently against the readers' background awareness of what is both communicatively conventional and linguistically normal non-literary discourse, i.e. both appropriate to the social purpose the message is to fulfil, as well as grammatically intelligible in terms of syntax and vocabulary. The unusually effective writings of poets, novelists and playwrights are thus 'foregrounded' against the familiar banalities of everyday language use, and so draw our attention first to themselves and thence to the unusual meanings they convey.

2.   The Primacy of Communication-Awareness and Language-Consciousness

The inevitable consequence of the foregrounding principle is that students of literature need above all else a gradual, patient and systematic training in how to read literary works. They have to be taught (i) how to recognize the special conventions that operate within the domain of literary communication in general, which are more often implicit than explicit; and (ii) how to go about making sense of the ways in which authors, especially poets, exploit the possibilities latent in the established code or system of the language in order to create and convey their own uniquely personal kinds of meaning. The first of these abilities enables students to assess and interpret the broader (and often more elusive) communicative effects of literary works in terms of how far, and in what respects, these either resemble or differ from the communicative conventions that govern the whole range of non-literary varieties of discourse. This ability might be rather crudely called 'communication-awareness'. The second might equally crudely be labelled 'language-consciousness', since it implies an explicit recognition of the need to look *at* literary language in order to discover its fullest meaning instead of looking directly *through* the language at a meaning which is self-evident. The latter is what happens, or rather what *seems* to us to happen, when we read the language of the commoner varieties of everyday written discourse in our mother tongue, such as news reports and journalistic articles, personal or official letters, instruction pamphlets and manuals, etc. Both kinds of ability are thus rooted in well-developed habits of comparison and contrast which already exist at an intuitive, pre-conscious level in every educated adult native user of a language. The study of literature demands that these habits be first raised to the level of full consciousness and then practised regularly in such a way as to make them habitual once more, but still conscious and explicit.

Communication-awareness is a complex matter requiring much more detailed exposition than is possible in this paper, whose readers must go to the works of Leech,[4] Chapman,[5] and Widdowson[6] for extended guidance on the subject. It is of the utmost importance to ESL literary studies since ESL readers of English literature are almost certain to miss much of the significance of what they read, if they are exclusively confronted with samples of literary writings but have little or no previous acquaintance with the styles of a wide range of non-literary types of discourse, spoken as well as written. Such readers can have little sociolinguistic sense of how the communicative function or purposes of these condition not only *what* the speaker or writer is likely to say but *how* he is likely to say it. One tiny example may give some hint of just how important such matters are in literary studies. If we read a poem which somehow reminds us of a prayer, it is not sufficient merely to note this as a vague impression. We have to ask in what precise respects it resembles the vocabulary and syntax of an actual prayer but in what other respects it differs from any authentic instance of real prayer, and why. This is because it is not an actual prayer but the artistic representation of one and thus a *fiction*. What sort of fiction it is will depend upon whether its style resembles that of private, personal and informal prayer uttered spontaneously, or that of the ritualized and predictable linguistic formulae of liturgy as used in formal public acts of religious worship. The answers to such questions are crucially relevant to how we interpret innumerable English poems, such as many of the sonnets of Shakespeare and Donne, Milton's *On the late massacre in Piedmont* Eliot's *Ash-Wednesday* and, more subtly, such very different poems as Wordsworth's *My heart leaps up* and Shelley's *Ode to the West Wind*. The whole communicative framework always has to be considered: who is addressing whom, in what circumstantial setting, on what topic, in what manner, and to what purpose. These are questions which students must be trained to ask themselves in relation to works in all the various literary kinds, genres and forms. It is all a matter of seeing the family resemblances — sometimes glaring, sometimes almost imperceptible — between the functional public styles of everyday discourse and the highly personal styles of creative writers. Above all, it is a matter of being able to describe both as accurately and as objectively as possible.

The same general principle of comparison and contrast applies to the smaller units of communication that make up the whole discourse — sentences, noun phrases, verbal phrases, adverbial and prepositional phrases. If students are to be able to interpret *for themselves* a creative writer's unusually effective uses of the language, especially those which subtly or even violently break the grammatical and semantic rules governing normal intelligibility, then they have to be made language-conscious through constant practice in the explicit comparison and contrast of unusual and unpredictable combinations of words with normal and predictable ones. Another very brief example must suffice here. Confronted with, say, Andrew Marvell's *The Garden*, students who are not trained in language-consciousness are either going to make anything they please or nothing at all of certain passages, unless their tutors gently compel them to make sense of Marvell's utterances by relating these to normal usage, both of the seventeenth-century and of the present day. The more celebrated and frequently-quoted the passage, the more likely are the students to misconstrue it or end up with only 'iceberg meaning' — the unsubmerged one-eighth of its significance that mere surface processing of the text makes apparent. let us take the notion of

> The mind . . .
> Annihilating all that's made
> To a green thought in a green shade. (43, 47–8)

Tutorial questioning might run along the following lines: What does the verb *annihilate* normally mean? How well do the dictionary definitions reduce to nothing and 'destroy the existence of something' fit the context here? Why don't they do so? Isn't it a grammatical problem? Does *annihilate* always demand a direct object? And can that direct object normally be followed by a prepositional phrase, i.e., *to* plus another noun or noun phrase? Would you write *The invading army was annihilated to a mountain of corpses* or *Science has annihilated faith to a phantom*?[7] Why not? OK, so if *annihilate* can't take a second, 'resultative' direct object after *to*, how do we have to read it here? We know that *annihilate* implies 'leave no residue' yet we have a residue here: *a green thought*, etc. Would you agree that Marvell's meaning is paradoxical, that it retains some of its conventional meaning of 'cause to cease to exist' but combines this with the unusual meaning 'reduce to X', cause to 'diminish to a mere remnant'? Surely these meanings would normally be mutually exclusive? So we have a unique 'value' or instantial meaning for *annihilating* here, one that occurs only in this poem.

And so the exploration would proceed, moving on to consider what is odd about the noun phrase *a green thought* in comparison with its more readily acceptable parallel, *a green shade*, and arriving at the conclusion that its combination of concrete adjective and abstract noun constitutes another unique and paradoxical semantic blend. What is unusually left over here after the mind has annihilated the whole of Creation (*all that's made*) is not a green object or substance as the language code demands, or even the mental image of a green 'thing', but simply the concept 'greenness', the *resemblance* or Platonic idea of greenness which is to be found, like the idea or image of everything else in created Nature, in the mind itself, as we are told earlier in the same stanza. The noun *thought* may then perhaps be extended to include the notion of meditation or contemplation, but this will of course depend entirely on how we interpret the whole of the remainder of Marvell's poem.

What emerges from such work is the recognition that the precise contextual value of every word, phrase, clause and sentence of a poem can be inferred only from its interaction with all the others in the text. More particularly the student learns that in many cases, this value is only partially determined by the rules of normal English usage, which (as here) may be radically flouted, and so depends on other, similar violations which combine to form a unified pattern of meanings which is unique to the poem in question. What is quite certain is that without this sort of training the student cannot utilize the historical erudition likely to be heaped upon him by his teachers and other scholars. All the knowledge in the world about the genre-conventions of pastoral, about the relevance of Renaissance neo-Platonism, and about possible 'sources' and influences can mean nothing to a student who is unable to construe the text and so discover what its meaning potential is. He can see the relevance of the scholarly information and select from it those bits which seem best to fit the unity of the poem only if he can react to its language in the ways this example suggests. Communication-awareness and language-consciousness are therefore complementary: neither is sufficient without the other, but initially the priority lies with language-consciousness.

In the end, of course, what matters most about the linguistic oddities of any literary text is the student's perception of how they cohere to form an overall pattern, or set of patterns, which is itself profoundly meaningful. Poets and other creative writers do not simply break the rules of grammar at random, or repeat the same grammatical structures over and over again out of habit, carelessness, incompetence or perversity. Their deviations from normal usage and insistent employment of some particular feature of syntax prove, on closer inspection than they commonly receive, to have special communicative value. They are not accidental but motivated and purposeful, their function being to give oblique expression to the theme of the work, the controlling notion or vision which the poet cannot express in the conventional language of everyday social necessity. Language is our way of representing the world to each other and must represent a common consensus of what that world is like, otherwise communication would break down entirely. The language of non-specialist discourse in the daily business of living can therefore only be agreed language, conventional utterances referring to our consensus world of commonsense factuality. In that world, as it is expressed by the English language, the sun 'rises' and 'sets' (though we have known for nearly five hundred years that it does no such thing), darkness falls and the stars 'begin to shine', behaving in a manner that is dully predictable in comparison with those seen by Coleridge's Ancient Mariner:

> The Sun's rim dips; the stars rush out:
> At one stride comes the dark . . . (lines 199–200)

In the uncanny supernatural context of the arrival of the ship of Life-in-Death, the stars and the darkness are terrifyingly and suddenly animated, as if acting out of superhuman intention, by Coleridge's choice of the verb *rush* and the noun *stride*. These are matters of some weight in a poem in which a storm is presented as an avenging angel *on o'ertaking wings*, where ice-floes *growl, roar* and *howl* like a wolf-pack, where the sea becomes semi-solid and *rots* and *burns*, where the sun *peers* through gratings, the stars can *dance* and a ship can *bound* like a horse. All of these are immensely important in a poem which has the sanctity of all modes of life, even the most repellent, as one of its major themes. Students are not immediately aware of such patterns. They have to be taught to recognize their presence before they can perceive their significant contribution to the whole work.

3. The Need for Communicative Competence in ESL

Mother-tongue students of English literature who have been made aware of the principle of foregrounding and have been taught in such a way as to develop personal communication-awareness and language-consciousness might be said to have acquired some measure of *literary competence*: the ability to read a work of literature by bringing into play the necessary presuppositions and implicit understanding of how literary discourse works that tell them how to read and what to look for.[8] The notion of literary competence is analogous to and based upon the more general concept of *communicative competence,* This is a convenient umbrella phrase which denotes the remarkable capacity that any native speaker of a language has for understanding utterances in it that he has never heard before as soon as he hears them spoken or reads them in print or handwriting. In the spoken medium (though not in the written) this is a capacity shared to a remarkable degree by any normally intelligent child of the same nationality who is under five years of age, provided always that the meaning of the utterance is one which is within his experimental range of understanding. Consider the following: 'Well, go and ask Mr Jones nicely if you can go in his garden and get your ball back.' Now although the child has never had a single formal lesson in how to use his native language he is in fact capable of performing instantly the following complex series of acts:

1. Dividing what is actually a continuous speech stream or sound-continuum into separate words which he recognizes as denoting persons, things, processes, etc.

2. Sorting the whole word-sequence into different groups which he recognizes as having different grammatical functions which he simply would not understand if someone were to call them 'subject', 'verb', 'object', etc.

3. Recognizing from the sequence of these word-groups that the speaker is uttering a directive, not making a statement or asking a question.

4. Understanding fully what this utterance counts for in the given context, i.e. grasping that he must confront an adult neighbour whom he may know to be of uncertain temper with a request which he, the child, has had to make before and which has not been well received (or whatever happens to be the case in the specific context-of-situation).

This striking ability to recognize and understand the structure, meaning and contextual implications of language-in-use depends upon knowledge which is entirely *implicit*, based on no analytic knowledge about how language works. The child's knowledge of the relevant communicative procedures and grammatical rules is completely internalized and he acquires it purely empirically through the trial-and-error of daily experience. The sheer practical need to communicate and to understand what others are saying and why they are saying it results in learning through constant exposure and practice-in-use. We learn to communicate in our mother tongue in the very act of doing it, gradually learning to exchange with others messages which are increasingly complex and sophisticated and doing so because the sheer pressures of existential necessity compel us to do so.

It would seem that we probably learn how to understand literary messages in much the same way, instinctively recognizing, however, that they do *not* arise out of necessity in the way non-literary messages do. The latter arise out of the inevitable compulsions of social interaction in the home, the neighbourhood, the community, the nation as a whole. Literary messages are not absolutely necessary in the same way, however desirable we may feel them to be, and this is a fact which is insufficiently explored and explained in most literary education. What is literature? What does it do, and how does it do it? These are questions which seldom figure in any secondary school or university literature course, yet upon the answers to them rests our whole orientation to literary modes of communication. Just as we are exposed to language-in-use from early infancy to primary school age so we are exposed at a later stage to written stories, poems, and dramatized fictions. Here too we seem to pick up instinctively, by trial and error, an implicit model or theory of what literature counts for as a very special kind of communication, gradually learning to approach literary messages with a set of presuppositions and expectations which are related to, but different from, those we use in coping with the linguistic messages of everyday life. If we did not have an internalized 'model' or theory of normal communication, an ability to interpret speech sounds and assign correct grammatical structures and appropriate situational meanings to them, our mother tongue would be an incomprehensible stream of gibberish to us. In a similar way we are first of all exposed to actual instances of literary discourse. Little or nothing is done by way of explaining to us precisely what is involved, even at quite senior levels of secondary education and even in university courses. It would therefore seem that we do form an internalized theory of interpretation which enables us to approach literary texts with at least some of the appropriate kinds of attention and ability their understanding demands. If this did not happen in some measure, none of us would be able to make any kind of sense of a poem or a novel in our own native language. Nevertheless the difficulties experienced by very many students of literature in *seeing the point* of the poems, plays and dramas they read suggests that teachers of literature have not yet done nearly enough to make conscious and explicit the nature of the interpretative presuppositions and procedures that are required for adequate interpretation of the works in question, even where the literature being studied is part of the students' own native culture and composed in his own mother tongue. Hence the importance of communication-awareness, language-consciousness and recognition of the foregrounding principle.

From all I have said up to this point it must be obvious that wherever the literature to be studied is *not* in the students' mother tongue they must already have a thoroughgoing proficiency in the use of that language. To get anything at all from serious works of literature by major authors, they require a communicative competence in the foreign or second language which is as close as possible to that of a highly eductated native user of it. This obviously goes far beyond the extremely rudimentary linguistic equipment often described as a 'reading knowledge' of the language — a mere operational grasp of its basic syntactic patterns plus a limited 'active' vocabulary and a passive one only slightly less limited and much more vague in terms of dictionary definitions and contextual values. For as I have tried to show, literary communication-awareness and literary language-consciousness both depend upon the principle of comparison and contrast, the first necessitating a developed awareness of the conventional public styles or registers of non-literary discourse and the second demanding the ability to interpret grammatically abnormal utterances by reference to and adjustment of the rules governing normal grammatical and semantic intelligibility. Without this solid background in the normative uses of English, the ESL student of English literature will be unable to perceive literary foregrounding, either in its socio-stylistic dimension or its syntactico-semantic manifestations. If he does not know what personal prayer or public prayer in English sound like in speech or look like in print, he will not recognize the prayer-like implications in poems which imitate prayer, or merely contain subtle echoes of prayer, or are parodies of prayer for comic, satiric or other literary purposes. And the same goes for a whole mass of non-literary varieties of discourse in English which the creative writer is free to imitate, parody, echo, and above all, mix up together in ways quite impossible in normal communication. Moreover if the student merely remains inert and uncomprehending when confronted with *a green thought* or, worse still, imagines it is a specimen of standard educated English that he may take over for his own use in any communicative context whatever, he will never begin to understand Marvell's *The Garden* and indeed should never have been required to do so. This is why the infection-theory of teaching the language through the literature is an absurd delusion, for literature itself presupposes by its very nature a command of the language so complete that it forms the background against which the reader interprets the writer's deliberate and significant deviations both from the norms of communicative behaviour, which produce unorthodox discourse, and from the rules of grammar, which produce abnormal and interpretation-resistant sentences. Besides being a special discipline in its own right (even when the trainee-readers are native speakers of English), the acquisition of literary competence demands communicative competence as its essential prerequisite.

The implications of all this for what is so often done under the name of teaching English literature in ESL countries could not be more serious. They are in fact so extensive that I can only outline a few of the more important ones at the end of this half of my paper. Meanwhile, there is another important sense of the word *language* which needs to be considered in connection with literary studies in ESL.

4. The Need for Analytic Skills and a Critical Metalanguage

Unlike private readers, students of literature are accountable for their reactions to the works they read. They are confronted with a selection of prescribed texts and are required to account for their reading experience of these works in term-papers, essays and examinations. In theory at least these tasks are intended to do rather more than merely reveal whether or not the students are superficially familiar with the works prescribed for study, i.e. have scanned the texts and abstracted in each case the general drift of the work, its plot outline or argument, plus impressionistic images of its characters etc. The tacit assumption is that such operations are designed to test whether or not the students have acquired certain literary abilities of an interpretative and evaluative kind. This assumption in turn presupposes one or the other of two conditions: either (a) that their academic instructors have actually taught them these abilities by some sort of transfer of skills, or (b) that continuous and repetitive exposure to literary texts in itself somehow confers these abilities on the students — two motions to which I shall shortly return. For the moment let us just consider what this student accountability entails. Reading experiences are inevitably subjective, so interpretations are likewise inescapably subjective. The only object factors in the whole situation are the texts of the poems, novels, plays, etc. Texts, however, are not in themselves works of literature: they are simply the reader's means of access to them. The words on the paper remain mere words on paper until a reader actively engages with them as intelligently and as sensitively as his knowledge of life and his command of the language will allow — and we have already seen what that implies. The reader has to reconstruct or re-create his own version of what the author hopes to convey by means of language. The work itself is thus an ideal or abstract entity — a potentiality that might be fully realized by some Ideal Reader. Meanings in literature are not to be instantly perceived in a ready-made state but must be actively recreated by the reader. The work is thus the result of the joint efforts of the author as an imaginative verbal artist or 'composer' and the reader as verbal interpreter or 'performer'. This analogy with musical performance is meant to be suggestive rather than exact, for musical notation and sounds do not refer to anything beyond themselves, whereas language refers to the extra-linguistic world. In reading a novel or a poem, therefore, the reader has the task of 'realizing' or imaginatively reconstructing the highly idiosyncratic version of that world created by the author's language. It is in this sense that he has to 'perform' the work sensitively if his reading experience is to be equal to the interpretative demands the writer's language makes upon him. It is his reading which brings the work into 'existence' as a mental or psychological event.

How then is the student to demonstrate the adequacy of his subjective responses to the objective linguistic facts of an author's text? It is a commonplace that literature does not simply engage the intellect alone but involves our emotions, our moral imagination and sense of values. Responses and interpretations are therefore likely to be highly complex during the actual reading process. How is the adequacy of a student's re-creation of any work to be assessed? How, for that matter, is he himself to describe it in terms which have any inter-subjective validity? Readers who are lazy, insensitive or perverse may claim acceptability for the most grossly inadequate and distortive of interpretations so long as subjective impression remains the sole criterion of adequate reading. How are such interpretations to be refuted? Once again a large part of the answer lies in the known facts of how the English language works for normal communicative purposes of the non-literary kind. The comparative/contrastive principle, both in its broader sociolinguistic aspects and in its narrower syntactic and semantic ones, is the teacher's public court of appeal and the student's guide to the interpretation of foregroundings and deviations—to say nothing of the less obvious linguistic features which may affect our interpretation of a literary text. Any authentic impression a reader derives from such a text must ultimately be traceable to some aspect of the author's use of language to create a unified literary discourse, the understanding and appreciation of which is the whole *raison d'être* of literary studies.

So, to be able to discuss his subjective reading experiences in anything other than subjective terms, a student of literature needs more than the ability to express himself fluently and congently in acceptable English of the appropriate kind. He needs a critical 'metalanguage' which will enable him to talk and write accurately about those linguistic and stylistic features of his prescribed texts which lead him to interpret them as he does. In any literary work but more especially in poetry, the author's use of English is likely to be deliberately and unusually effective, so that the student will be facing the most fundamental of literary-critical questions: 'Given these words in this order, what gives them the powers they have?'.[9] To answer it, he must be able to relate the creative writer's linguistic innovations to the much more predictable and conventionally appropriate English of everyday non-literary discourse, as our examples from Marvell and Coleridge have shown. In other words, he needs an *analytic* knowledge of how the English code or language system conveys the kinds of meaning that it does when used for the purposes of mundane practical communication. The information he needs for these purposes is in fact readily available. It is to be found in the new, communication-oriented reference grammars of English published in the past decade, in recent manuals of descriptive rhetoric, and in the pedagogical approaches to literary stylistics proposed in the writings of H. G. Widdowson and others.[10] The advantages and incentives of such an approach to literary studies are immense, especially in ESL countries. For if the majority of ESL graduates in English are to teach the use of English to school pupils, then this analytic competence in the language is precisely what they need if they are to explain the relationships between grammatical structures on the one hand and the communicative purposes they serve in actual use on the other. Moreover, if they go about it in the right ways they will indeed be able to extend their pupils' language skills by teaching literature in the way its peculiar nature demands that it be taught, namely as an extension of the skills and abilities needed for ordinary purposes of communication in English.

5.   The Need for Pedagogic Dialogue

Everything said so far implies that students will never learn to understand literature if left to themselves to read literary works in the same way as they read newspapers, magazines and textbooks. Nor will they acquire the special skills and abilities required for literary competence if their classroom role is that of mere passive receptacles for information and received critical opinion doled out *ex cathedra* in lectures. The fundamental purpose of a literature course should be to teach students how to discover literary significance for themselves in the very act of reading. Furthermore this must be done by methods which will enable them to 'extrapolate', i.e. carry over and apply the interpretative principles and procedures learned in reading one set of texts to the interpretation of others, in the same genres, which are new and unfamiliar. This implies guidance and control by the teacher, which in turn necessarily implies *dialogue* between teacher and student.

Given only conventional lectures and left to confront his set texts alone, no student can ever be certain that his subjective re-creation of any drama, novel or poem is adequate to the demands its structure and texture actually make upon him. As a result he tends to take over and profess the opinions of those critics he is taught to regard as prestigious. Being inexperienced and unsure of himself, he cannot possibly know whether his own interpretations are valid or not, especially if they remain unexpressed and entirely private to himself. The only way in which he can learn whether they are feasible or even relevant is through active participation in discussion. The subjectivity of personal reading experience has to be offset throughout his whole course of instruction by inter-subjective exchanges of interpretative opinion with his teachers and fellow-students. Moreover if such exchanges are to be more than the mere airing of surmises and prejudices they must focus as consistently as possible on the only objective factor: the precise linguistic form of the author's text, which establishes both the scope and the limits of its potential significance. If this dialectical dimension is missing from the course, no student can develop a genuine literary competence, and indeed nothing worthy of the name of literary study is taking place. It follows that the essential teaching device is not the monologue of the informative-evaluative lecture but the dialogue of the seminar or tutorial group discussion. Here, under the teacher's direct guidance and control, subjective impressions can be exchanged, verified or modified, enriched and finally pooled in a genuine co-operative effort to arrive at the optimal interpretation of the work—one in which the greatest number of subjective responses is correlated with the largest number of demonstrable textual data, without the intrusion or irrelevances, the omission of crucial evidence, or the loss of that interpretative consistency which seeks to account for the unity of the work.[11]

It is in such discussions that the individual student gradually develops his personal literary competence and learns to use the concepts and procedures of literary stylistics. Here he will need his analytic knowledge of the language system and of the conventions according to which non-literary discourses vary in style according to their communicative functions, for this is also where he must employ his awareness of 'foregrounding'[12] and of the comparative/contrastive principle to validate or enhance his understanding of the working under discussion. It is in such discussions, and in preparation for them, that he will learn not merely to perceive recurrent patterns in vocabulary and syntax and sound but to understand what they contribute to the whole communicative effect of the work. Certainly he will need to be instructed in all this by means of demonstration lectures in which interpretative procedures are exemplified and stylistic devices are identified, named, and explicated, preferably in the context of a short work rather than in isolation. Lectures of this sort lend themselves admirably to question-and-answer dialogue between lecturer and class—a mode of teaching insufficiently exploited, in my opinion, in university literature courses. But unless he is compelled to use all this, however tentatively at first, in regular and frequent seminars focusing on 'unseen' works, the student may treat the details of grammar and descriptive rhetoric as just another set of facts and labels to be hastily mugged up for some examination which treats them not as means to literary insight but as ends in themselves. He must be made to think of them as means, as the essential tools of his trade which he can only learn to use with skill and sensitivity through continual patient practice in interpretation. Only through tutorial group discussion will he learn to use them to explicate both the communicative effects of linguistic deviation and those aspects of an author's language which, precisely because they are not deviant, may seem to him too trivial for serious interpretative attention. As I hope to show in Part II, such unobtrusive textual features may in fact be of crucial thematic significance.

6. How Not to Teach English Literature

The five principles or conditions roughly outlined above have negative corollaries far too numerous to be dealt with here. Let me simply suggest some of the things that happen when the principles are not borne in mind, as they frequently are not in ESL countries. Most ESL teachers of English literature are genuine ambilinguals who use English as fluently as they do their mother tongue. Many of them therefore suffer from the 'language-blindness' that afflicts too many native speakers of English who are involved in the teaching of literature. The educated native user's high level of communicative competence all too commonly means that the last thing he is interested in is how his mother tongue works, especially outside the literary domain. He therefore tends to be interested only in literary discourses and disdainful of any close and systematic concern with how they are expressed, believing that grammar is a dully prescriptive pedantry about when to use *whom* instead of *who* and how to avoid split infinitives and prepositional endings to sentences. Properly understood, grammar — in the widest sense of the word — is the dynamics of communication, and we teachers of literature ignore it at our peril. But many ESL teachers of English literature hold views similar to those of the educated native speaker of strong literary interests, and for the same reason: they enjoy a highly proficient but wholly internalized communicative competence in English. In recent decades, however, their students have increasingly been drawn from non-bilingual homes and backgrounds where English is not well taught in school and where there are few environmental inducements to use it outside the classroom or the lecture theatre. As a result, students of pitifully low proficiency are often exposed to thoroughly institutionalized 'Eng. Lit.' degree syllabuses modelled on archaic British ones. These include no continued training in the use of English, no training whatever in analytic competence (i.e. the elementary linguistics and sociolinguistics of modern English) and nothing remotely resembling systematic training in literary competence as I have loosely tried to define it. In its place one sometimes finds 'Critical Theory' — the rote learning of gobbets from Sidney's *The Defence of Poesie*, Coleridge's *Biographia Literaria* etc, for ritual regurgitation in answer to separate examination questions on this topic. Classroom dialogue scarcely exists, for too often the sole mode of instruction is the information-loaded lecture, while the sole mode of sadly belated feedback is the end-of-session examination script.

The consequences are unedifying. Grossly underequipped for the long, difficult and complex task which (in theory) confronts them, large numbers of students never have any personal experience of prescribed works, even if they attempt to read them. The *texture* of these august masterpieces remains opaque and baffling, so the student has not personal access to their deeper implications, i.e. their thematic structures as literary works. However, what might be called their 'surface' literary structures, i.e. their extractable plot-lines and poetic arguments are readily accessible. These works have, after all, been discussed in print for many generations. Consequently convenient synopses and paraphrases, off-the-peg interpretations, predictably acceptable evaluations and an impressive range of encomiastic formulae can be assembled from lecture memories (students seldom make undictated notes), prescribed critical reading, and the plethora of lucrative study guides marketed by some of the more economically enterprising but less academically illustrious former alumni. The inconvenience of having to process the text and experience the work at first hand is thus completely obviated. So, of course, is the entire point of a degree course in literature: learning how to become a competent reader, not merely of a set of prescribed works but of any literary work in English.

I feel sure I need not elaborate on the dire educational consequences of all this, either in terms of the immediate outcome in the form of examination results or with regard to their longer-term repercussions on the teaching of English in the very schools from which the students are drawn. Many academics across a wide range of ESL countries are increasingly aware of these issues, but are either uncertain about how to put matters right or prevented from doing so by time-hallowed but misguided educational traditions and the entrenched academic conservatism of elder bureaucrats. Part I of this paper has offered these teachers some points of argument which they may find useful if temporarily disturbing. Part II is intended as a microsample of what might help to fill the vacuum that so often exists where the teaching of literary competence should be.

PART II: Interpreting a 'One-Image' Poem

IN A STATION OF THE METRO
The apparition of these faces in the crowd;
Petals on a wet, black bough.

Ezra Pound (1913)

These twenty words constitute one of the best-known miniature classics in Anglo-American poetry of the present century. How might one set about helping ESL students to experience its meaning as fully as possible? In what follows I suggest a number of questions one might put to them so that the significance of the poem should emerge from their own grapplings with the meaning potential of the linguistic forms which make up the title and text. Practical stylistics start from the ability to account for the communicative effects of the simplest and most normal language features such as definite v. indefinite article, plural v. singular noun, simple v. complex NP (i.e. noun phrase) and so on, rather than from an exclusive preoccupation with attention-riveting figures of speech and blatant deviations from normal usage. Superficially at least, there is nothing notably deviant about this tiny poem, but of its total of twenty words only nine are 'content' words (seven nouns and two adjectives) while the remaining eleven are so-called 'function' words — articles, prepositions and a demonstrative adjective. These crucially affect the impression any text makes on us, especially when they account for more than half of a poem as short as this one. This is why the following explication may seem unduly concerned with the minutiae of grammatical structure and the rhetoric of ordinary non-literary communication, both written and spoken. I offer no apology for this. The simplest linguistic patterns are often the most difficult to explain when they are used to powerful literary effect. Moreover, in handling the poem in these terms I shall seldom be able to describe in full the various grammatical and semantic 'rules' involved since that would leave little room for the interpretation itself.

Wherever necessary I shall simply refer my readers to readily available reference works which deal with these matters in detail, in the hope that they will consult these in testing the validity of the interpretation I suggest here.

I have implied that one ought to proceed mainly by posing textual questions for the students to try to answer. The careful sequencing of these is obviously important but sometimes difficult to maintain in a classroom discussion. Also, different poems are likely to demand different starting-points, so I would emphasize that there is nothing prescriptive about the sequence in which various points are handled here. I do not believe, however, that tutors should launch straight into formal linguistic questions since these are likely to distract the students' attention prematurely from a poem's communicative impact as a whole. Personal experience has convinced me that the initial question should always be a very general one, such as: 'What do you make of this after two or three attentive readings?'. Without initial guesswork of this kind on the part of every student in the class, genuine personal literary competence can be neither taught nor acquired. No matter how vague or inept students' first impressions may be, they are the indispensable basis for discussion of the kind that leads to an optimal interpretation.

First impressions of what the poet is 'saying' will not be forthcoming, however, if the students lack information which the poet has assumed to be shared by himself and his readers. In an ESL teaching context, different poems will once again demand different kinds and different amounts or preliminary clarification in this respect. Even these matters of presupposed information should nevertheless be made the focus of questions whenever possible, perhaps in the form of 'research' questions issued before the practical stylistics class meets. Meanings discovered personally are always more compelling than raw factual information doled out hastily in class. In the case of Pound's mini-poem, these preliminaries are essential to a proper understanding of how and why the poem communicates what (in my opinion) it does.

Preliminaries

The crucial question here is simply: 'What do the words *the Métro* refer to?' Obviously it is important for students to understand this as a reference to the underground railway system of Paris. Because of the way the poem works communicatively, however, it is even more important for them to understand that the Métro of 1913 was a dank and gloomy place. For students with no experience of underground railway stations the tutor may even have to describe one, emphasizing its least attractive features. A first step toward a more formal approach to the poem's significance can then be taken by asking: 'Why was anyone unlikely to ask "Which Metro is the poet talking about?".' This should focus attention on the use here of the definite article plus a colloquially abbreviated and capitalized adjective to refer to a geographically unique 'thing' or referent. Several benefits should arise from this. It should help to clarify the difference between what single lexical items ('content' words) *denote* in the dictionary and what they *refer to* when combined with a determiner and used in a particular context-of-reference. It will also reveal that when an adjective is used with the definite article as the name of some public institution, it takes on the whole denotative burden of the discarded noun it originally modified – in this case, the common noun *railway* converted to the partial proper noun *Railway*. Above all, it will alert students to the context-sensitive way in which articles, demonstratives and other determiners confer on their nouns meanings which are either specific or non-specific, whether the article is definite or indefinite and even when there is no article at all. The absolute uniqueness of reference in the case of *the Métro* will be confirmed if the tutor adds that the equivalent colloquialisms elsewhere in the English-speaking world are *the Tube* and *the Underground* in Britain and *the Subway* in the USA.[13] With these preliminaries out of the way the tutor can begin to elicit first impressions of the poem's impact on individual students.

Analysis

The obvious starting-point is the context-of-reference – what the poem is about. At this early stage the tutor would be wise to insist on a fairly 'literal' approach to identifying the predominant subject-matter or topic of the poem. In particular, premature attempts to label the whole piece as a comparison, simile or metaphor should be politely resisted until a number of more basic issues have been settled. One might well begin to focus attention on formal features by inviting comment on the title, which in form as well as function is not unlike a dramatist's printed stage-direction setting the scene for an immediately forthcoming action-cum-dialogue. Earlier discussion of the unique reference carried by *the Métro* has already established the wider context as a real one, but the communicative effect of the indefinite singular noun phrase *a station* is still to be assessed. The concept of 'shared knowledge' can once again be invoked to clarify this. Is the poet assuming that we, his readers, already know which particular Métro station is the immediate setting for what follows? Most students will rightly think he is not, and the point can be reinforced if we invent the contrastive title *In the Métro Station* as a possible alternative which, without fully identifying the particular station in question, nonetheless pretends that the reader knows which one is being referred to. In this connection one may usefully point out that Pound revealed elsewhere that he had based his poem on an experience he had in the underground station at the Place de la Concorde.[14] Why, then, did he not identify the station fully in the poem? Guided consideration of this question should lead students to conclude that for the purposes of the poem the precise identity of the station is irrelevant. It should be pointed out that, taken in isolation, the indefinite singular phrase *a station of the Métro* is inherently ambiguous in meaning. It could be either (a) a so-called 'generic' reference to any Métro station whatsoever, or (b) a specific reference to one particular station about to be more fully identified in the ensuing text.[15] Now no such identification occurs in the body of the poem, which neither makes explicit mention of the Métro nor names the station. Nevertheless students will readily agree that line 1 gives the impression of a highly specific occasion and therefore of a uniquely particular location. The meaning of *a station of the Métro* in this context is thus an unusual blend of generic meaning (any Métro station) and specific meaning ('this/that particular Métro station')—a fact which should lead students to conclude that what matters about this station for the poet and consequently for us is not its unique identity but rather its typicality of its class or kind—the Métro stations of Paris, certainly, but possibly all stations of this type. Thus in bringing up the biographical point about the Place de la Concorde, the tutor will incidentally but very usefully have demonstrated that 'evidence' from outside the text itself, even when provided by the author, is not always relevant to interpretation and may even be positively (if unintentionally) misleading. It is always the precise language-form of the text that is the essential clue to a poem's significance, rather than those factual details the author's private life which inspired its composition.

The students' impression that line 1 gives expression to some unique experience may now be investigated in relation to what we already know about the title. How, one might ask, would we interpret line 1 in the absence of any title? If we were to ask ourselves which apparition is referred to, we should be forced to reply 'The one consisting of faces', and if we then asked 'Which faces?' we should find ourselves replying 'The ones in the crowd', But then, of course, we should be compelled to ask, finally, 'Which crowd?' —and without Pound's title we could propose any sort of crowd we cared to think of. The reason for this is essentially a grammatical one which the class should be made aware of. In each of the NPs *the apparition, these faces* and *the crowd*, the determiner is a definite one making a specific reference. In all three cases, however, that determiner is a forward-pointing one. This means that the definiteness of the determiner indicates that the identity of the thing denoted by its noun or headword is established by the qualifier, i.e. the postmodifying element which immediately follows that noun, as in *the underground stations of Paris*, where *of Paris* identifies which stations are meant. In line 1, however, the three determiner + noun structures are all related 'in depth', in a complex type of structure sometimes called 'embedding' or 'depth-recursive rankshift'.[16] This can be shown by bracketing of the kind which distinguishes between the two potential meanings of an ambiguous noun phrase such as *old men and women*. Thus the bracketing

((old men) and women)

restricts the scope of the adjective *old* to the noun *men*, whereas the alternative

(Old (men and women))

extends the scope of *old* so that it modifies both nouns. Treated in the same way, Pound's first line requires to be bracketed as follows:

(The apparition (of (these faces (in (the crowd;)))))

Unlike *the apparition* and *these faces*, however, *the crowd* has no qualifier to identify it. To understand which crowd, and indeed what sort of crowd, we have to relate that singular definite reference retrospectively to the title, which is another (but simpler) structure of the same type:

(In (a station (of (the Métro.))))

We might even say that readers mentally add this grammatically unattached prepositional phrase to the end of line 1, using the same device of 'Chinese box' embedding or rankshift to form the following long, complex nominal group:

(The apparition (of (these faces (in (the crowd (in (a station (of (the Métro.)))))))))

The massive amount of bracketing entailed arises from the fact that all *of*-genitives[17] and other prepositional phrases contain within themselves either a 'bare' noun or a noun phrase which is capable of functioning independently as the subject, complement or object of a clause containing a predicator (i.e. verbal phrase or group). In prepositional groups these are 'downgraded' to function as complements to their prepositions.

There is one slight danger in accounting for the identification of *the crowd* by means of that final, enormous bracketed nominal group; it may mislead students into thinking of the title as part of the utterance made in the body of the text, instead of as an authorial signal to the reader, as is any actual scene-setting stage direction.

A more conventional way of identifying the referent of *the crowd* is to handle it in terms of lexical cohesion.[18] This is simply to treat the whole work as a printed text written for silent reading, noting that in the context provided by the title, the unqualified singular definite reference, occurring as the first mention of any crowd, is identifiable in terms of the high probability of its co-occurring with groups like *The Métro, a station*, and of course *these faces*, in some other bit of discourse, such as the gossip or fashion column by the Paris correspondent of a British newspaper or indeed any casual conversation in English about people seen in the Métro. For of course this linguistic tendency among the nouns *Métro, station, crowd* and *faces* to collocate depends upon the frequency with which the non-linguistic referents of these words co-occur in actual situations. This explanation avoids the danger of students assuming that they are to 'hear' the title in the same way as they are expected to hear (or overhear) the utterances made in the two lines of the text proper—a point to which I shall revert later.

Before leaving the matter of the definite article-plus-noun groups which occur in line 1, the tutor might ask those who feel strongly about the 'unique experience' effect of line 1 to pick out just what it is in the wording of the text that convinces them of the appropriateness of their response. One might even ask the rather devious question: 'What tense is the poem written in?' since this will alert even the less astute members of the class to the fact that there are no verbs at all in this text. In turn this should focus the attention of the more talented students in the *these faces*. This is different from *the apparition* and *the crowd*, which though definite, are neutral as to relative distance or proximity in time as well as in space. Here is the true source of any feeling that the time-setting of the text is the immediate present and that the faces are the ones I see here and now, quite close to me.' For as a determiner, *these* is maximally specific, suggestive of immediacy in space and/or time, and above all, selective:[19] it picks out certain faces for special attention, faces which are close rather than distant. Temporary substitution of *those* for *these* will clinch this point. Some students may nonetheless resist the notion that only certain faces are being selected as being of special interest here. The tutor should direct their attention to the implications of the qualifier *in the crowd*, which presents the crowd as a given area or mass within which certain faces attract special attention from the observer. Temporary substitution of feasible alternatives will confirm this point also. Had Pound written *the faces of the crowd* or even *the faces of this crowd*, his poem would have been a very different one, saying something about the whole collective mass of faces.

The selective demonstrative *these* is a key item for yet another reason: it confers upon the two other definite article groups in line 1 the function of outward-pointing references to situational data, to things immediately visible in the speaker's environment at the moment when he utters these words. We have already seen how *the apparition, these faces* and *the crowd* function as textual references, the first two pointing forward to their own qualifying phrases while the third points back by lexical association to the title. But in this context *these faces* is only secondarily an intra-textual reference. Primarily it is a situational one, for although there is nothing inherently odd about the occurrence of the noun *faces* along with *station, Métro*, and *crowd*, there is certainly nothing obligatory about its inclusion here. Given only the title, we do not necessarily expect any references to faces at all. The poem might have been about a deserted Métro station seen at three o'clock in the morning. This is the very first mention of faces, yet it is not only specific but selective, and not merely selective but 'near', not 'far', in its perspective in space and time. Consequently these here-and-now implications rib off on both *the apparition* and *the crowd*, which likewise take on the character of immediate situational references. This is why *these faces* is also the source of our feeling that *a station*, despite its indefiniteness, refers to a unique and potentially identifiable location. Its function within the title is to suggest any typical Métro station, but in the context of poem as a whole that typicality is combined with powerful implications of unique particularity. The uniqueness of the moment captured in line 1 demands a particular station as its setting, but that station remains nonetheless typical of its kind.

Having recognized the sources of the impression of present immediacy created by the interaction of line 1 with the title, the class should now be able to comment perceptively on the headword *apparition*, which dominates the first line. They have seen that the occurrence of *faces* in this context is marginally less predictable than that of *crowd* and that the sudden immediacy implied by *these faces* creates in the reader a mild degree of surprise. What would they now say about the likelihood or otherwise of the noun *apparition* occurring in such a context? One might tackle this from the situational end by asking the students whether apparitions are as commonly associated with crowded Tube stations as they are with such settings as the battlements of Elsinore and the bedchamber of Ebenezer Scrooge. Even the briefest consideration should lead them to conclude that the specific situational reference to an apparition should occasion even greater surprise, particularly as it is the first of such references in the text. At this juncture it would be instructive to replace *apparition* temporarily with the much more frequently used noun *appearance*. This should lead to a renewed awareness that *appearance* itself has two potential meanings which cannot be combined in normal, non-literary uses of this item. The first, which we shall call *appearance*[(1)], denotes an act of coming into view, whereas the second, *appearance*[(2)], denotes the visual impression someone or something makes on observers, the aspect or character presented by something or someone when seen. Since there are no verbs in Pound's poem to limit the substitute noun to one or other of these meanings, it would inevitably become an example of poetic 'ambiguity', or rather of multiple meaning, since both values of the word would be relevant to the poem. Even then, however, it would fail to capture the precise value that *apparition* takes on in this context. Dictionary entries for this noun should be consulted, but even the information that an apparition is essentially a 'coming into view, especially of a ghost or the spirit of a dead person' does not really provide us with everything we need in order to assign to this word the precise semantic value it takes on in this poem. For this our students will need to employ that combination of imagination and reason which the adequate interpretation of any poem demands of us.

As we have seen, the noun *apparition* essentially denotes an action and so includes the meaning expressed by *appearance*[(1)] but adds to it the further component of meaning carried by the adjective *supernatural*, which *appearance*[(1)] does not normally express. Furthermore, such an action implies an agent, which in this case is a supernatural being of some sort. So any non-literary use of the word *apparition* presupposes a very special and abnormal manner of coming into view on the part of a being whose aspect or 'looks' cannot be other than strikingly impressive, to say the least. So *apparition* automatically takes on the meaning of *appearance*[(2)] as well, but again with the additional adjectival meaning of *supernatural*, which *appearance*[(2)] does not normally express. Now the concept of the supernatural includes both non-human entities (gods, angels, demons, etc) and 'ghosts', i.e. the returned spirits of human beings known to be dead. As apparitions, both share certain basic attributes which violate the known laws of logic, causality and probability. By their very nature they are paradoxical, being visible yet non-physical, so that their actual 'being there' when seen is in doubt. Their visitations are sudden, startling and brief, and they disappear as inexplicably as they come into view. Not surprisingly, therefore, the word *apparition* tends to have connotations of fear, or at least awe, on the part of the beholder.

If we now ask which of the features normally attributable to an apparition seem attributable to the faces mentioned in the poem, the students probably begin by discarding that last one, for nothing whatever in the poem seems to suggest a frightening experience. The faces are obviously human ones, so we are not dealing with a non-human apparition. The qualities of suddenness, power to astonish and transitoriness are likely to be retained. So is visibility, obviously, but what about concreteness, substantiality? If the faces are those of formerly living human beings, i.e. ghosts then the situation is even odder than we may have thought it — not just one ghost seen amid the crowd in a busy Métro station, but several. If, on the other hand, *the faces* refers to living human beings, then we cannot invest the noun *apparition* with its normally obligatory component of meaning, 'non-concrete', i.e. non-physical. It would seem, therefore, that we have to read *the apparition* figuratively in this particular respect, while retaining certain other of its implications. Obviously the faces must seem transitory since the very choice of *apparition* as the dominant headword implies that their sudden, unpredictable appearance and disappearance, though in no way sinister, is surprising.

In a markedly different way, this feeling of surprise extends for readers of the poem to the whole content of line 2. We have been able to establish cohesive ties between the vocabulary items of the title and those of line 1 (except *apparition*), but no such lexical associations seem to tie line 2 to the rest of the poem. Whatever the nature of this apparition, its location is clearly inside the Métro station and not outside it, and the bough of a tree with petals on it cannot be part of the same scene since no tree could grow, far less blossom, in the subterranean tunnel of a tube station. Nor is there any ready connection to be made between a flowering tree and a supernatural phenomenon of some kind, whether involving the spirits of the human dead or not. Yet the two lots of entities are referred to within the boundaries of a single minor (i.e. verbless) sentence, a juxtaposition which clearly suggests that we are to seek some sort of meaningful connection between them, despite the fact that all the references of line 2 are indefinite whereas all three in line 1 are not only definite but point, as we have seen, to data in the speaker's immediate environment.

What, then, is the relation between the two complex nominal groups constituting lines 1 and 2? At this juncture the tutor should be ready to introduce the notion of semantic equivalence, a rhetorical device whereby the reader is encouraged to make unusual connections in meaning between language items which are syntactic equivalents because they occupy 'parallel' positions in the structure of closely related clauses, phrases, etc. in the same text.[20] Parallelism is of course not difficult to perceive in verse because the special lineation of the text tends to draw it to our attention. Now Pound's two lines, the tutor can point out, are not of identical rhythm and length, so the parallelisms are not immediately obvious. The crudest structural analysis of these two nominal groups there produces the following, where M = modifier(s), H = noun head and Q = qualifier(s), with the zero-symbol '0' marking any blank slot in one group which happens to be filled in the other:

> M   H   Q
> The APPARITION of these faces in the crowd;
> 0   PETALS   on a wet, black bough.

This does not seem very revealing in terms of structural and semantic equivalences. An abstract noun denoting a supernatural manifestation is here 'equated' with a plural common noun denoting concrete natural objects, namely flower-petals, while human faces seem to be equated with the saturated bough of a tree. Students should be reminded, however, of the complexity of the qualifier in line 1, which contains within itself yet another MHQ structure — the last one, indeed, in that line. Now the last MHQ structure in line 2 is in fact the first and only structure of that kind in that line, and if we match up these two we get the following:

> M   H   Q
> these FACES   in the 0 0 CROWD;
> 0   PETALS on a wet, black BOUGH.

The class may now begin to see rather more interesting possibilities of equivalence here. Two singular monosyllabic nouns denoting concrete things are matched up in the pair *crowd/bough*, which are also coupled by assonance in place of conventional rhyme. More significantly still, perhaps, two disyllabic plurals also denoting physical things are equated here, matching up things suggestive of some possible visual analogy between them: faces and petals. Quite rightly, however, some students will complain that this bit of analysis cheats because it leaves out something vital, namely the MH group *the apparition*, on which they have just spent a lot of time and which clearly dominates everything else in line 1. This should be instantly conceded, but with a reservation. Do we not frequently find elliptical structures in English,[21] sentences and clauses in which an important element of structure already released in one unit of the utterance is 'understood' and not repeated in a coordinate structure which immediately follows? And may not this be the case with our two coordinate NPs? Acceptance of this possibility results in a reading of the poem which we might represent as follows:

> M   H   Q
> The apparition of these faces in the 0 0 crowd;
> (The apparition of) 0 petals on a wet, black bough.

This makes *apparition* the dominating headword of both nominalized minor clauses and consequently the key lexical item in the work, for it means that we have to treat the notion of petals on a wet, black bough as being just as apparitional in quality, within the context of the poem, as the special faces in the Métro station crowd. Moreover, this reading solves the problem of the verblessness of the text which, together with the semicolon which indicates a clause boundary, prevents us from interpreting the first nominal group as subject and the second as subject-complement of a finite clause. No verb is needed, and indeed none that is adequate could be supplied from the lexicon of modern English, as our scrutiny of *appearance* (and by implication, its verbal root *appear*) has shown. If such a verb existed, it would have to be given a dictionary definition along the lines of *vb int.* — come into and pass out of view in the manner exclusive to supernatural beings. For as the class has already been shown, *apparition* is a noun denoting an action rather than a 'thing' and thus is always in need of an *of*-construction to identify what it is that carries out that action.

What our analysis has revealed is that Pound's poem sets up a four-term analogy in which, within the context jointly provided by the title and a 'shared' fifth term, *these faces* are to *the crowd* as *Petals* are to *a wet, black bough* — the shared term of course being that both are treated as having some, but not all, of the qualities of apparitions. This is why it is recommended that simplistic premature classification of the poem as 'a metaphor' should be resisted. It is a metaphor, but it is a complex one containing at least four figurative propositions:

1. Certain faces in this Métro-station crowd = an apparition.
2. Petals on a wet, black bough   = an apparition.
3. These particular faces   = petals.
4. The crowd in a Métro station   = a wet, black bough.

What the class must now discover are the grounds on which these equations are made. Here one might well start with *petals* and *faces*. How does the context limit the range of meanings we can assign to these? Indeed, how do they limit each other's meaning here? All petals are flower-segments but not all flower-segments resemble human faces. Similarly, the faces in question are certain faces picked out from the mass of faces forming a Paris tube-station crowd, and not all human faces suggest any analogy with flower-petals. It seems likely that we have to think of disc-shaped petals, and faces that attract special attention precisely because they resemble flower-petals in shape, colour and texture. Moreover, tube stations tend to be fairly dark places and in the Paris of 1913 were darker than they are now, so dense, dark or intense shades of colour seem inappropriate, especially since *apparition*, being most commonly applied to human ghosts, tends to suggest relative paleness at least, as well as being seen suddenly, surprisingly, and only so very briefly that one wonders whether they were real or not. Above all, the faces are likely to be those which suggest the beauty and delicacy of flower-petals.

Here the tutor might remind students that *petals* has no determiner whatever in the poem. If it stood absolutely alone it would be a pure generic plural denoting all the members of its class. In the poem, however, it receives some measure of identification from its prepositional qualifier. These are not just any petals but petals seen under stated conditions, when the bough on which they are located is both wet and black. That the bough is wet suggests either recent heavy rain or perhaps the wetness left behind by snow that has thawed. The second adjective, *black*, also seems to denote a temporary condition rather than a permanent attribute of the bough (though this is debatable), so that it is perhaps its extreme wetness which accounts for its blackness. When, one might ask, are petals likely to be seen under such conditions? This is, of course, a seasonal question which may create difficulties for some ESL readers. But a further difficulty arises which some students may themselves mention: is *petals* to be interpreted literally here, or as a synecdoche—a part-for-whole figure of speech? Are we to envisage detached petals or complete flowers? A definitive answer to these questions is probably not possible and may indeed be unnecessary, but the contextual probabilities should at least be explored.

Pound's reputation for meticulous craftsmanship would suggest that the literal reading is the more suitable one, the notion of detached petals being appropriate to an image of single isolated faces of delicate beauty but also of pallor, is implied by *apparition*. Students might be led to note that the most feasible lexical alternatives—*buds, blossoms, blooms* and the more general *flowers*—all seem too 'healthy' by comparison, being at odds with the rather spectral aspect of the faces glimpsed in the unnatural gloom and polluted air of a tube station. This reading suggests a somewhat pessimistic vision of faces analogous to 'dashed' petals left sticking to the bough after an end-of-season rainstorm. On the other hand, if *petals* is a synecdoche (chosen perhaps more for the light sounds of its unvoiced /p/ and /t/ than for denotative precision) then we may be being invited to imagine emergent buds dotted here and there on a bough wet with melted snow or spring rains. In this case the vision is a more optimistic one implying that even in the worst and seemingly least probable circumstances, beauty can startle us with its unpredictable but brief visitations. One should emphasize that in either case *a wet, black bough* has to be analogically matched with *the crowd*. The two adjectives certainly apply to the tunnel walls of a tube station and may well extend here to the dark (and rain-soaked?) clothing of the crowd which cannot but conform to the hollow 'branch' shape of their surroundings.

Some students will inevitably point out that the two interpretations proposed are incompatible, suggesting that one must opt for one and discard the other. What I want to suggest here is that we are not forced to choose and that both kinds of significance can be accommodated with the poem. This depends upon the time-scale on which we interpret *apparition* in relation to the two different images. The specific situational references to a unique occasion in line 1 clearly suggest a momentary vision of beauty in the Métro station and therefore a very narrow time-scale. The setting is urban, non-natural and, by implication, inimical to natural human beauty. The image in line 2 is exclusively natural, with probable seasonal implications of an ambiguous kind. Here *apparition* figuratively denotes an annually recurrent phenomenon: the blooming of a flower-bearing tree, with everything that implies about a duration of days or even weeks. In the context, however, this image takes on all the semantic features with which *apparition* has already invested *these faces*: unexpectedness in context, near-incredibility, association with death and, above all, brevity of duration. The lifetime of flowers on a tree is reduced to the same duration as that of an instantaneous glimpse of beautiful faces in a tube-station crowd. But the very same analogy also reduces the lifespan of a beautiful person to that of a single flower, the poignancy of this device being sharpened by the implication that these faces are seen in unnatural and adverse surroundings. Yet at the same time, the blossoming of a tree is a cyclically recurrent event, so there may be a hint that the Métro-station kind of experience, though rare, may also recur – hence the typicality of the indefinite singular reference *a station*. The pathos of the brief life of all natural beauty, human or floral, is sharply emphasized if we interpret *petals* literally, for then the image is of a beauty already dying or dead. If we read *petals* as a part-for-whole figure, the emphasis is on beauty's inevitable recurrence. Beneath these alternative perspectives, however, the implications remain the same for faces and for flowers alike: the species continues, but the individual member is inescapably mortal. The only difference is the implication that the worst aspects of the man-made urban environment are likely to destroy human beauty proportionally faster than nature inevitably destroys its own products.

A few final questions can be raised, mainly to corroborate points already made. What, for example, is the communicative effect of the contrast between the markedly specific situational references in line 1 and the indefiniteness of those in line 2? We already know why the latter cannot be outward-pointing and we know, too, that there is no lexical cohesion of the normal kind between the nominal groups in these two lines. The only meaningful connections between them are those suggested by the parallelism we have just explored. In that scheme of analogical equivalences *these faces* demand a matching plural, which we found in *petals*. In the same way *the crowd*, being an immediate situational reference, demands a singular equivalent. It would therefore seem that the overriding reason for the indefiniteness of *a wet, black bough* is the need for singularity of number and not the wish to refer to some particular bough. The tutor should point out that the adjectives *wet* and *black* do not here identify some particular bough which happens to be the one the speaker is talking about. They merely specify the temporary state in which we are to envisage an otherwise unidentified bough with petals on it. In other words, *a wet, black bough* as used here is a generic reference, but of the 'typical instance' kind and not the inclusive 'whole species or class' kind.[22] Moreover, since the headword *petals* have no determiner at all this typicality characterizes the whole HQ group. Any instance of petals on a bough that is wet and black will serve the speaker's communicative purpose, which is not to refer to some given instance but simply to evoke a concept or mental image of what these words typically denote. Plurality throughout (*petals on wet black boughs*) would be a general use meaning all instances: Pound's nominal group is a 'concretized universal'. The result is that the poem directly relates the situational data of a unique, non-recurrent moment of human and urban experience to the details of a universalized image of a perennially recurrent event in non-human 'Nature'. Because the two are analogically fused or assimilated to each other by being treated as if they were both supernatural, our conventional ways of thinking about both are disrupted and we see them in new ways and new relationships which are both revealing and moving. And that, the tutor can point out, is the basic function of all new metaphor.

Much has now been said about the poem's context-of-reference but little about its possible context-of-address. Now there is an obvious sense in which every poem is a one-way written discourse intended for silent reading and addressed by the poet to the world at large. But the texts of poems (as opposed to their titles) commonly carry implications of spoken utterance. They are nearly always artistic imitations, or partial imitations, of speech. Moreover, the voice we hear in a poem frequently is not the voice of the poet in his own person but the imaginary voice of some other person or thing whose identity he has adopted. Similarly the person addressed in the implied context-of-address is quite often not the reader but some imagined *dramatis personae.* How does 'In a Station of the Métro' strike the class in this respect? The tutor might point out that syntactically free-floating nominal groups are thoroughly uncharacteristic of continuous written discourse, which in any case seldom consists only of a title plus a single minor sentence. Does the text (i.e. lines 1–2) therefore seem closer to a spoken utterance made 'on the spot' by the observer of the arresting faces in the Métro-station crowd? To whom is it likely to be addressed? Discussion of this is likely to lead to the conclusion that any real remark made to a friend or fellow-passenger might be just as elliptic in form but would never be either so unusual in content or impractical in function. Nor is it easy to envisage the observer uttering these words aloud in self-address in the middle of a thronged tube station! It would seem, therefore, that the text is characteristic neither of one-way written discourse nor of two-way face-to-face conversation, nor even of talking to oneself. This seems to be a written text which does not set out to represent speech at all, but to represent perceptions as immediately and directly as possible. As students should see without too much difficulty, this has the important implication that the experience the poem records is an entirely subjective impression — an event in the mind of the perceiver. Furthermore, because of the absence of first person pronouns (*I, me*) and possessives (*my/mine*), the experience becomes that of every reader, who himself 'becomes' the perceiver at the moment of reading.

The fact that the grammatical impersonality of the text places every reader in the role of experiencer of the 'apparition' is closely related to three other textual features already noted: (i) the proximity in space and time suggested by *these faces*; (ii) the complete absence of finite verbs and therefore of tense-carried reference to time; and (iii) the underlying twin themes of generic survival v. individual transience and mortality. The first two features combine to lift the experience out of actual time, locating it in an idealized present moment which recurs at every reading. The beautiful faces, fugitive in two different senses, are perpetuated along with the delicate and still more fleeting petals. The poem, as artefact, paradoxically immortalizes the beauties it simultaneously celebrates and mourns. The extreme elliptical brevity of the text not only replicates their intrinsic transience but that of the instantaneous flash of insight in which the two become one thing, with the result that the moment of revelation is itself perpetuated.

This extreme condensation of message was an effect the poet strove to achieve during a year in which he gradually reduced an original draft of thirty lines to the poem as we now have it. He also suspected that this 'one-image poem', as he called it, might be meaningless to readers unaccustomed to the mode of thought its interpretation demands. What I have offered here is an attempt to account for that mode of thought in terms of the communicative possibilities latent in the linguistic facts of the text. All I claim for my interpretation is that it is as consistent with those facts as I can make it. Some readers may have found the procedures by which I arrive at this interpretation unnecessarily tedious. In reply I would simply say that it is only by asking ourselves questions of the kind exemplified here that we can hope to validate our interpretations of poems at all. If, as teachers of literature, we cannot so validate them, we can only impose our interpretations on our students. If we do that, they will never learn how to account explicitly for their own reactions to the poems we make them read. Only by helping them to become conscious of the interpretative processes themselves can we enable students to interpret poems adequately and validly, without help from us or from other intermediaries between them and the meaning potential of the texts.

References

1. G. N. Leach, *A Linguistic Guide to English Poetry*, (LGEP) Longman, 1969, pp.1–3.
2. *LGEP.*
3. H. G. Widdowson, *Stylistics and the Teaching of Literature*, Longman, 1975.
4. G. N. Leach, *English in Advertising: A Linguistic Guide of Advertising in Great Britain*, Longman, 1966, and *LGEP.*
5. Raymond Chapman, *Linguistics and Literature: An Introduction to Literary Stylistics*, E. Arnold, 1973.
6. H. G. Widdowson, *op. cit.*
7. An asterisk placed before a sentence or phrase indicates that it would be unacceptable according to standard usage.
8. For a discussion of literary competence see Jonathan Culler, *Structuralist Poetics*, Routledge & Kegan Paul, 1975, pp.113–30.
9. I. A. Richards, 'Poetic Process and Literary Analysis' in T. A. Sebeok (ed.), *Style in Language*, Cambridge, Massachusetts: The MIT Press, 1960, p.11. This essay and

Richard's other contribution to this volume, 'Variant Readings and Misreading' (pp.241–252) are strongly recommended.

10. Grammars include R. Quirk *et al., A Grammar of Contemporary English*, Longman, 1972, and two associated manuals: R. Quirk and S. Greenbaum, *A University Grammar of English*, Longman, 1973, and G. N. Leech and J. Svartrik, *A Communicative Grammar of English*, Longman, 1975. The last named is particularly suitable for undergraduate work in ESL. Among rhetorical manuals, G. N. Leech's *A Linguistic Guide to English Poetry*, Longman, 1969, is indispensable. H. G. Widdowson, *Stylistics and the Teaching of Literature*, Longman, 1975, is essential reading for all concerned with the pedagogical principles and practices touched upon in the present paper.

11. On 'optimal' interpretation see *LGEP* pp.214–21.

12. See *LGEP* chapter 4, 'Foregrounding and Interpretation', pp.56–71.

13. The Moscow Underground did not exist when Pound conceived and wrote this poem. The marble splendours of any of its main stations would be an inappropriate setting for the 'epiphany' embodied in the poem, as my comments on *a wet, black bough* may suggest.

14. Ezra Pound, *Gaudier-Brzeska: a Memoir*, The Marvell Press, 1960, pp.86–9. See also Cleanth Brooks and Robert Penn Warren, *Understanding Poetry*, 3rd ed., New York: Holt, Rinehart & Winston, 1964, pp.88–92.

15. See Leech and Svartvik, *A Communicative Grammar of English*, on definite and indefinite meaning, sections 69–77. Further references to this work will identify it simply as *CGE*.

16. For explanations of the terms Depth, Recursion and Rankshift see J. McH. Sinclair, *A Course in Spoken English-Grammar*, Oxford University Press, 1972, glossary and references to the text; the entries under Nominal Group, Modifier, Headword, and Qualifier also provide useful definitions and refer to samples analyzed in Ch. 3 of this systemic-descriptive grammar.

17. See *CGE*, sections 95 and 96.

18. Lexical cohesion can be loosely defined as the way in which repeated or associated vocabulary items give unity to a discourse. This, however, is only one kind of cohesion. A very full treatment of the subject will be found in M. A. K. Halliday and Ruqaiya Hasan, *Cohesion in English*, Longman, 1976, hereafter abbreviated to *CIE*.

19. See *CIE*, section 2.4, on demonstrative references; also *CGE*, sections 88 and 89, especially on outward-pointing uses of demonstratives.

20. See *LGEP* pp.62–9 and elsewhere as indexed.

21. For ellipsis, see *CGE* on 'omission', sections 390–409.

22. See *CGE*, section 74; also *LGEP* pp.193–4.

STYLISTICS AND THE TEACHING OF LITERATURE

M. H. SHORT

University of Lancaster

1. Stylistics and Criticism

The sub-discipline of stylistic theory and analysis, with its application of linguistic methodology to literary texts has existed in its present form for some 15 years.[1] Yet in spite of its usefulness in literary analysis it is still ignored by a majority of teachers of English Literature. The reasons for this are manifold, but important contributory factors are: (i) The difficulty for literary scholars of learning the new linguistics. (ii) The general post-Leavis assumption that in order to react properly to literary texts readers have to belong to a largely pre-existing category of 'sensitive' readers. According to the Leavisites, sensitivity is encouraged by exposing students to good works of literature and getting them to like them. Hence their tastes are trained to conform with those of the literary establishment. Those who fail to like or understand fall by the wayside and join the insensitive, underprivileged majority. (iii) The feeling that literature is a 'subjective' phenomenon and therefore cannot properly be analysed by 'objective' linguistic analysis.

The first of the three reasons, although an important practical consideration, cannot be regarded as academically serious. If a case can be made out for the inclusion of stylistc analysis in criticism, then any serious critic must knuckle down to it, no matter how alien he finds the mode of analysis. The second reason, however, bears more examination. Firstly, it rests on an assumption that literary texts are different from other examples of language. This view is usually supported by the assertion that writers of (good?) literary works use language creatively, but the rest of us do not. Hence it is thought that poetry, unlike other kinds of language is full of metaphors, images, patterning, rhetorical tropes etc. But the examination of other kinds of language e.g. advertising, political speeches, belies this distinction; even casual conversation in the coffee bar can produce new metaphors. Indeed, no objective comparison of literary with non-literary texts has been able to hold a linguistic line between;[2] and given the fact that modern poets have taught us that excerpts from newspapers, when placed inside volumes of poems, must be regarded *as* poems, the recent view of writers like Stanley Fish[3] and Mary Louise Pratt[4] would seem most judicious, namely that a text becomes a literary text just because we choose to regard it that way. This is in line with the other arts; a sunset can on one occasion be treated as a meteorological phenomenon from which weather predictions can be made, and on another as an object of aesthetic interest. Similarly, a metaphor that would pass unremarked in a notice becomes self-valuable if it occurs in a text labelled 'poem'.

The arguments for and against treating literature as like or unlike other kinds of language are of course more complex than this brief sketch would suggest. Nevertheless, I believe the 'no distinction' view to be essentially correct. If it is, it follows that the notion that literature is the reading preserve of the 'sensitive' becomes untenable and the problem of the less sensitive reader who does not understand some poem or poems cannot be swept under the carpet. I am not, of course, suggesting that sensitivity is not required to understand and enjoy good literature, but merely that such sensitivity is in principle teachable to a much wider range of readers than seems to have been hitherto supposed. Consider the first stanza of 'yes is a pleasant country' by E. E. Cummings:

> yes is a pleasant country;
> if's wintry
> (my lovely)
> let's open the year[5]

A sensitive reader might quickly glean the following interpretation (I omit the other two stanzas on purpose so that 'context' does not at this stage interfere with the reader's judgement): the *persona* in the poem is addressing his loved one, and is arguing that her saying 'yes' to him will produce a warm (summery?), pleasant condition for them both; but if she tries to stall him with conditions ('ifs') the result will be unpleasantness. Hence at the end of the stanza he explicitly asks her to say yes.

A teacher with intuition but no linguistic analysis to help him would appear to be reduced to helping the 'insensitive' student by reading the text to him again, perhaps with special intonation and stress placement (a kind of ostensive definition) and by making more detailed assertions like '"pleasant country" has connotations of warmth in this stanza' in order to carry his student with him. And this may indeed help; but if it does not, it is difficult to see how further explanation can take place without recourse to linguistic analysis, which, let us note, can provide more detailed and explicit support for the reading suggested. First, the first two lines are semantically deviant: '— is a pleasant country' demands the name of a country as subject, and '—'s wintry' requires a subject which is capable of being made cold. *Yes* and *if* obviously do not meet those requirements. Hence the first two lines of the poem have to be interpreted non-literally. Moreover, the two lines are syntactically parallel. They both have a subject-verb-complement (SVC) clause structure, where the verb is *is*, the subject is a 'grammatical' word, and where the complement has connotations of pleasantness or unpleasantness. This structural parallel is important, as parallelism invites readers to perceive a connection between the two lines so that they are linked semantically as being 'the same' or 'opposite' in some way (as opposed to vaguer relations like 'different').[6] It is this feature of parallelism which invites us to view 'pleasant country' as warm. Pleasant countries do not have to be warm, as visitors to northern Europe will know, but in this poem they are.

It should be apparent that whatever meaning is arrived at for the whole poem, it will have to have non-literal interpretations for the first two lines which are also in some sense opposed. The meaning which I suggested above satisfies these requirements. Moreover, the presence of a vocative in the third line of the stanza and the *invitation* speech act[7] in the last line presuppose a discourse situation for the poem where one person is addressing another; and the lexical content of the vocative indicate a lover-loved relationship. The last line of the poem also contains a semantic violation in that 'let's open the —' would normally require a noun or noun phrase referring to a physical object which can be opened. Hence this line also needs a non-literal interpretation, one which will do justice to the line and also fit in with the rest of the poem. An explanation which takes these factors into account is that the lover is inviting the loved to say 'yes' and make love. If an agreement has been entered into, the participants must in effect have said yes. Notice that it follows by inference that the opening of the year is warm, pleasant, and probably springlike. Again, literally this does not have to be true; in the northern hemisphere January and February are cold winter months. But the pressure to produce consistency of interpretation in the poem leads us to associate the beginning of the year with spring (the nearest warm season), with its connotations of youth and growth, rather than the real beginning of the year.

It should be clear that all of the linguistic features I have pointed out together support the interpretation originally suggested. It may not be the only possible interpretation, of course, and the reader may have thought of alternatives; but whatever other explanation is put forward will have to take into account the foregrounded linguistic features which I have mentioned.[8] Other readers may wonder why I have bothered to go into such detail on such a perfectly obvious piece of poetry. The reply to this is, I think, that although the meaning may be obvious to you it may not be to others; and a fairly simple example of the role linguistic structure plays in interpretation is the clearest way to illustrate the use of stylistic analysis in all cases. Showing 'insensitive' students how texts acquire the meanings they do seems the only possible way of getting them to appreciate them once pointing and assertion have failed. Moreover, it would also seem a sensible idea to show students both of literature and language the role that language plays in moulding their views. For it is a short step from making readers of poetry believe, even momentarily, that pleasant countries have to be warm, to persuading the general populace to take on board undesirable views. Showing how persuasion works in literature will make students more aware of how it works in so-called 'everyday' language.[9]

There is, however, another motivation for going into the relationship between linguistic structure and interpretation, namely to demonstrate the centrality of stylistic analysis for criticism. Literary studies embrace a wide range of activities — biography, the relationship of a text to its historical and cultural milieu, the relationship between a text and another work to which it alludes, and so on. But these activities, although interesting and valuable in themselves, would appear to be ancillary to the central critical task of understanding and judging literary works. I see the core of criticism as consisting of:

1. Evaluation
   ↑
2. Interpretation
   ↑
3. Description

Evaluation is what every textual critic must be working towards. But note that very little is known about how we decide intersubjectively to rate works as good or bad. Indeed, twentieth-century literary criticism has tended to concentrate on the middle area, interpretation, to the exclusion of the rest. Critics have vied with one another to produce a plurality of interpretations for the same work. In one sense this is not surprising; for evaluation logically depends upon prior interpretation (the arrows in the diagram above indicate dependency relations). Level 1 depends upon previous analysis from level 2, which in turn depends upon analysis at level 3. It makes no sense to say 'this is a good/bad work, but I don't really understand it'. It should also be noted, however, that interpretation depends upon a logically prior level of *description*, which in the main will be *linguistic*. In order to understand a sentence one must first of all have scanned it syntactically and lexically, for example. And to understand the metaphors in the Cummings' poem we must also perceive the clauses as being deviant or 'untrue' in order to go on and frame non-literal interpretations for them.

In spite of the fact that linguistic description is prior to interpretation, critics have tended to ignore it. This is one of the major reasons for the production of relatively large numbers of interpretations for the same text. The check which stylistics (which selects stylistically relevant linguistic features and relates them to interpretation and effect) has on the framing of interpretations has largely been absent, fostering plurality and hence the general view that literary criticism is essentially subjective.

This brings us to the third of my suggestions as to why criticism has on the whole ignored stylistic analysis, namely because of the view that it misapplies objective analysis to a subjective phenomenon. First let us note that whether 'literature' is subjective or not is a meaningless question and irrelevant to our present concerns. The important matter is whether or not criticism is subjective. It must of course be acknowledged that because we have, each of us, grown up with a personal set of experiences, various words may have special associations for us and so on. But even if the word 'wintry' does mean something special to me, that does not mean that it cannot also have a range of meaning which I share with other individuals in my speech community; in fact people often explicitly recognize such a distinction, saying things like 'dustbins have a special meaning for me — I met Mary when I tripped over one in Surbiton'. And in any case, one of the lessons to be learnt from our examination of the lines from 'yes is a pleasant country' is that in some particular text even (perhaps especially?) variable aspects of meaning like associations of words are controlled by textual structure. Moreover, if, as I have suggested earlier, there is no good *linguistic* distinction between literary and non-literary texts, the subjectivity hypothesis would push us into saying that *all* texts must be understood differently by each individual. Perhaps this is also true, but it appears less commonsensical. When my wife and I read a leader from *The Times* or listen to the news on the radio, we do not appear to differ much, if at all, in our understanding of what is said. Indeed, if we did, it is not obvious how communication could take place at all. But then I also seem to understand much the same by 'yes is a pleasant country' as my students, a not surprising situation when the foregoing analysis is taken into account. Whatever different interpretations are put forward will have to account for linguistically verified features of the text which are stylistically relevant. This applies as much to poetry as to any other kind of text. In other words, criticism, by concentrating on interpretation rather than the kinds of arguments and evidence which could be brought forward to support or invalidate particular interpretations have tended to raise differences between readers at the expense of acknowledging how much they share.

I suspect that another reason for the opposing of the objective (science) to the subjective (humanities) is a common misunderstanding of what it means to be objective. The layman often appears to think that to be objective means to discover eternally verified truths, and that the hard sciences are the disciplines where such truths can be found. The problem with this view is that even physicists disagree and change their minds, often for what might seem to be odd reasons for the layman — for economy, for example. One of the important reasons why Newtonian physics were replaced by Einsteinian physics was that the latter's account could include the former's within a more general and more simple framework. In other words, to choose between the theories one of the important things to take into account was the general set of 'rules' and conventions which govern argumentation. This works for interpretations theories?) of texts too. If we are to choose between two interpretations which cover the text equally well, the less ramified will win. Thus one of the things involved in being objective is to make one's analyses as explicit as possible and subject them to the general canons of argument. To be sure, critics cannot repeat experiments in the way that scientists can, but their discipline, if it is to be regarded as a discipline, must have accounts which are open to verification and refutation. Being explicit about how we get to the interpretations that we do, which will necessarily involve stylistic analysis, would be a large step in the right direction.

It is not surprising, once critics have hoodwinked themselves into believing that the meanings of texts have great variability, that there has been a widescale movement on their part away from textual analysis and towards more ancillary modes. For it could only be in such modes that they could meet in true academic argument. It is instructive that the most well-known collection of articles on Joyce's — *Portrait of the Artist*[10] devotes a third of its space to papers discussing Joyce's aesthetic theory in relation to the novel, and that many of the other contributions are only concerned with the text in this indirect way. Again, let me reiterate that such contributions must have a place within literary studies, and that some critics do involve themselves more directly in textual analysis.[11] But in general the trend within the British and American universities is that of a covert 'flight from the text', a flight which, if criticism is to achieve a proper balance and eventually account for the fact that some texts are more highly valued than others, must be reversed.

2. Teaching English Literature Overseas

In fact the 'flight from the text' has been even more marked in the teaching of English Literature overseas than it has been in England and America. My experience when visiting foreign universities has been that there is a larger emphasis on teaching courses on the history of criticism, the historical and social background to Shakespeare's plays, and so on. In a sense this is not surprising; if the English critic has 'gone ancillary' then it is likely that his counterpart overseas will have followed suit, especially when we consider that his problems are considerably multiplied. It has been argued, for example, that because Wordsworth's 'I wandered lonely as a cloud' cannot be understood unless you know about daffodils and the Lake District, the English teacher must spend some of his time filling in the gaps. I am sure that this is to an extent true. But concentration on more text-immanent features must be even more crucial in the teaching of second language literature because the 'sensitivity' problem is made worse by the fact that the overseas student is unlikely to have a sufficient grasp of the norms of the language to be able to determine what is deviant, foregrounded, and hence crucial to understanding.

It was a lack of appreciation of the importance of deviant linguistic structures in understanding which was largely responsible for the failure of the more traditional attempts to teach English language *through* English literature. Exponents of this view felt that the best way to teach English was to expose foreign students to the greatest exponents of that language, namely its great poets, novelists and dramatists. But in order to understand 'yes is a pleasant country' one needs to know (a) *that* it is deviant, and (b) *how* it is deviant before one can even begin to frame an interpretation for the line. And in order to know that it is deviant one must know the norms of the language, a knowledge notoriously difficult for the foreign learner to acquire.

Should one remove literature from the English syllabus overseas then, as many ESP approaches have done? I think not. Especially in more advanced classes, students enjoy good literature even though they may understand it somewhat imperfectly. And the older students get the more resistant they are to learning grammatical rules by rote etc. The interest value alone would seem to be an essential area to tap; and via detailed stylistic analysis it should be possible to explain to foreign students how meanings and effects come about in poems etc. even if they do not perceive them at first sight. Indeed, it would seem even more important to provide the foreign student with explicit analysis than the native learner; otherwise he has no reasonable access whatever to a sensitive appreciation of the text concerned. Moreover, such analysis, as it depends upon the explication of norms via grammatical analysis etc., will also serve to teach the student about the structural characteristics of English or some variety of English from which a particular text deviates or to which it aspires. In other words, by teaching him how meanings arise in specific instances, the English teacher has a powerful, double-edged tool. By showing how meanings come about he increases enjoyment of and sensitivity to good literature; at the same time he increases the student's explicit awareness of the general norms and conventions governing English usage. And we should remember that the foreign student has one very positive advantage over his English counterpart, namely that he is familiar, through long-term exposure, to linguistic terminology and analysis precisely because the teaching of English grammar (unlike in England) has never been expunged from the foreign learner's curriculum. This means that he is better prepared to cope with the detailed technicality of stylistic description so necessary for him to increase his understanding and awareness. But even if this were not the case it would still seem to me that the arguments for explaining, via stylistic analysis and other such tools how particular texts acquire particular meanings through the applications of the general conventions of use, are stronger when teaching English literature overseas than at home, precisely *because* the chances of a student misunderstanding are greater, and because the only way of guaranteeing with any certainty that misunderstandings are cleared up is through as explicit an analysis as possible.

3.   Stylistics and Criticism—An Example from Joyce's *A Portrait of the Artist as a Young Man*

So far the examples I have used have been from poetry. To conclude this paper I will demonstrate the relationship between sylistics and interpretation and effect by an extended (though by no means complete) analysis of a prose passage, namely the evocation of the epiphany which Stephen experiences in *A Portrait of the Artist as a Young Man* when he sees the girl on the seashore (Penguin edition, pp.171–2). An epiphany for Joyce is a moment when an abrupt spiritual awakening is experienced in which thoughts, feelings, attitudes etc. cohere to produce a new and sudden awareness:

By an epiphany he meant a sudden spiritual manifestation, whether in the vulgarity of speech or of gesture or in a memorable phase of the mind itself. He believed that it was for the man of letters to record these epiphanies with extreme care, seeing that they themselves are the most delicate and evanescent of moments. (*Stephen Hero*, I, p.211)

In this particular epiphany the vision of the girl on the seashore acts as the final catalyst which makes Stephen decide to replace a religion which has become increasingly meaningless and unreal by a belief in life and art:

1.   There was a long rivulet in the strand and, as he waded slowly up its course, he wondered at the endless drift of seaweed.(1) Emerald and black and russet and olive, it moved beneath the current, swaying and turning.(2) The water of the rivulet was dark with endless drift and mirrored the highdrifting clouds.(3) The clouds were drifting above him silently and silently the seatangle was drifting below him and the grey warm air was still and a new wild life was singing in his veins.(4)

2.   Where was his boyhood now?(5) Where was the soul that had hung back from her destiny, to brood alone upon the shame of her wounds and in her house of squalor and subterfuge to queen it in faded cerements and in wreaths that withered at the touch?(6) Or where was he?(7)

3.   He was alone.(8) He was unheeded, happy and near to the wild heart of life.(9) He was alone and young and wilful and wildhearted, alone amid a waste of wild air and brackish waters and the seaharvest of shells and tangle and veiled grey sunlight and gayclad lightclad figures of children and girls and voices childish and girlish in the air.(10)

4.   A girl stood before him in midstream, alone and still, gazing out to sea.(11) She seemed like one whom magic had changed into the likeness of a strange and beautiful seabird.(12) Her long slender bare legs were delicate as a crane's and pure save where an emerald trail of seaweed had fashioned itself as a sign upon the flesh.(13) Her thighs, fuller and softhued as ivory, were bared almost to the hips, where the white fringes of her drawers were like feathering of soft white down.(14) Her slateblue skirts were kilted boldly about her waist and dovetailed behind her.(15) Her bosom was as a bird's, soft and slight, slight and soft as the breast of some darkplumaged dove.(16) But her long fair hair was girlish: and girlish, and touched with the wonder of mortal beauty, her face.(17)

5.   She was alone and still, gazing out to sea; and when she felt his presence and the worship of his eyes her eyes turned to him in quiet sufferance of his gaze, without shame or wantonness.(18) Long, long she suffered his gaze and then quietly withdrew her eyes from his and bent them towards the stream, gently stirring the water with her foot hither and thither.(19) The first faint noise of gently moving water

broke the silence, low and faint and whispering, faint as the bells of sleep; hither and thither, hither and thither; and a faint flame trembled on her cheek.(20)

6.   —Heavenly God! cried Stephen's soul, in an outburst of profane joy.(21)

7.   He turned away from her suddenly and set off across the strand.(22) His cheeks were aflame; his body was aglow; his limbs were trembling.(23) On and on and on and on he strode, far out over the sands, singing wildly to the sea, crying to greet the advent of the life that had cried to him.(24)

8.   Her image had passed into his soul for ever and no word had broken the holy silence of his ecstacy.(25) Her eyes had called him and his soul had leaped at the call.(26) To live, to err, to fall, to triumph, to recreate life out of life!(27) A wild angel had appeared to him, the angel of mortal youth and beauty, an envoy from the fair courts of life, to throw open before him in an instant of ecstasy the gates of all the ways of error and glory.(28) On and on and on and on!(29)

(Both paragraphs and sentences are numbered for ease of reference)

The main burden of my analysis will consist of an examination of the way in which Joyce manipulates point of view and the presentation of Stephen's thoughts in the passage. I will also try to show that the moment of epiphany suddenly occurs in sentence 21. But first I would like to try and sort out a critical disagreement over the sexuality of the description. Jane H. Jack believes Stephen's perception of the girl to be sexual as well as aesthetic:[13]

> In the most profound moment of his youth he portrays himself near 'the wild heart of life'. The erotic imagery is identical in significance with 'the seaharvest of shells', the arid grasses and the earth. The word mortal is used twice of the girl he finds wading. The word grapples sex to life and therefore to his art.

Richard Ellmann, on the other hand describes the girl as Stephen's 'secular correlative of the Virgin Mary',[14] and Eugene M. Waith supports the 'unsexual' view:[15]

> Profoundly moved, but not sexually aroused, he looks at her for a few moments, then turns away and strides off across the sand . . . Stephen has 'fallen' in that he has taken a beautiful body as an object of contemplation instead of the religious mysteries with which he occupied his mind after his confession and communion, yet his excitement is what he is later to describe as 'the esthetic emotion' . . . Instead of plunging Stephen again in the mire of sensuality, this 'fall' advances him toward the artistic goal he envisages.

I would like to support Ellmann and Waith in opposition to Jane Jack. First of all, the evidence which Ms Jack advances is not particularly convincing. There is no obvious reason why the seaharvest of shells, arid grasses or the earth should be erotic. Moreover, *mortal* does not have inherent sexual connotations, and in both the expressions in which the word occurs ('the wonder of mortal beauty, her face'(17), 'the angel of mortal youth and beauty'(28)) it is collocated with *beauty*. In the first instance it premodifies *beauty* in a phrase which itself postmodifies *wonder*, the whole phrase being in apposition to *face*. In the second case it premodifies *youth* and *beauty* in a phrase postmodifying *angel*. Sexual descriptions do not usually concentrate on girls' faces or angels, and it is significant that the second instance of *mortal* occurs in a paragraph of 96 words in which *life* is repeated three times and the verb *live* occurs as well. This would seem to indicate a more standard interpretation of the word, as having to do with the living as opposed to the immortal. Its collocation with *angel*, which occurs twice in the same sentence also supports this view. Mortality appears to have more to do with the right to err and sin, and hence is opposed to the Catholic proscription which Stephen rejects. In sentence 27, 'to live, to err, to fall, to triumph, to recreate life out of life', *to live* and *to recreate life out of life* are paralleled with verbs to do with the opposing notions of falling and triumphing. In sentence 28 *error* is also co-ordinated with, and hence paralleled to *glory*, a synonym for triumph. Mortality is thus strongly associated with the set of words to do with sin, error and triumph.

Is there any other evidence which could be brought forward to support either view? Nouns like *bosom* and *thigh* do appear in the description of the girl in paragraph four. But they are overtly associated, like many other aspects of the girl's description, with birds by the explicit use of simile. Moreover, the paragraph is structured so that we move up the girl toward her face. The subjects, and hence topics, of the main clauses, in order, are *a girl, she, her long slender bare legs, her thighs, her skirts, her bosom, her long fair hair* and *her face*. The sequencing involves a progression, with the face occurring in the final, climatic position at the end of the paragraph. The head is the only part of the girl's body which is referred to by two topic phrases. An examination of the syntax of the final clause of the paragraph 'and girlish and touched with the wonder of mortal beauty, her face' also supports the view that the girl's face is the most important part of her. If we produced a 'normalized' version of this clause, we get 'and her face was girlish and touched with the wonder of mortal beauty'. It is thus obvious that the clause is transformationally rearranged in order to foreground *face*. It occurs in the end-weighted position in the sentence and also as the final word in the paragraph. Thus the evidence of inter- and intra-sentential sequencing, with its evidence on *face* confirms the lexical evidence indicating that the description of the girl is aesthetic rather than sexual.

The discussion above provides an example of how concentrated attention to relevant linguistic evidence can help to decide critical disagreements. I now want to move on to examine Joyce's manipulation of point of view in the passage. However, in order for the reader to follow the argument he will have to be familiar with stylistic theories of speech and thought presentation.

In particular, my analysis rests on the account of this area put forward in Chapter 10 of *Style in Fiction* by G. N. Leech and M. H. Short,[16] to which the reader should refer if the following shorthand account is unclear. I give a brief description of the account here as it differs in significant ways from earlier work in the field.[17]

Besides the categories of Direct Speech (DS) and Indirect Speech (IS) which a writer has available to him, he also has the possibility of using Free Direct Speech (FDS) or Free Indirect Speech (FIS). Examples of the four types are:

1.   He said that he liked it there in Bognor. (IS)

2.   He said, 'I like it here in Bognor!' (DS)

3.   I like it here in Bognor! (FDS)

4.   He liked it there in Bognor! (FIS)

In speech presentation (in this case direct character speech in the novel) what was said in one speech situation is reported in another. In DS the distinction between the two discourses (i.e. (character—character) vs (narrator—addressee)) is made clear by the distinction between the report*ed* and the report*ing* clause, the former being marked off within inverted commas and being relatively independent syntactically. The reported clause also contains linguistic features appropriate to the embedded speech situation. Hence, if present time is referred to, the present tense is used along with near time- and place-deictics (see the present tense and the adverb *here* in 2 above). The other linguistic levels mights also be appropriately marked; for example colloquial lexis and indications of the phonological character of utterance might be used. In our example the exclamation mark is a graphological indication of intonation and tone of voice. If the speech is reported in the indirect mode (IS) then the reported clause becomes grammatically subordinated to the reporting clause, and the features originally appropriate to the embedded speech situation will change to suit the higher one. The most common type of novel narration, and that which occurs in *A Portrait of the Artist* is relatively formal, third person, and past tense. Hence in our examples the present tense in 2 becomes past in 1, the near deictic *here* becomes the remote *there* and the exclamation mark is omitted. Free Indirect Speech (FIS) is a hybrid of DS and IS. In our example 4 the subordination of the reporting clause associated with IS is missing and the exclamation mark associated with the more direct form is retained; but the tense and deixis are appropriate to the non-embedded speech situation. Free Direct Speech (FDS) has the reported clause of DS, but may omit either or both of the features which indicate the presence of a narrator, namely the reporting clause and the quotation marks. Our example 3 gives the most extreme form. The four modes of speech presentation are distributed along a cline which moves from a situation where the character's words are apparently given verbatim, without any narrative interference to one where the formulation of the utterance is apparently completely under the control of the narrator:

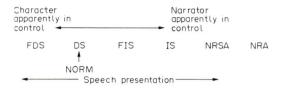

In FDS and DS we are told what the character said in the words that he used. In IS we are told what the character said, but in the narrator's words. FIS is a hybrid between the two. Moreover, as DS is the norm for the presentation of speech, the use of FIS is usually perceived by readers as indicating narratorial intervention. It is thus often used for distancing, irony, or both.

But in order to understand the functions of the modes of speech presentation we need to relate it to Narrative Report (NR) via the Narrator's Report of Speech Acts (NRSA):

5.   He expressed his pleasure at being in Bognor. (NRSA)

6.   He liked Bognor. (NR)

The narrative report of events, scenes etc. are obviously completely under the control of the narrator. The narrator's report of a speech act is the verbal equivalent of the report of an act. This can be seen by comparing sentences like 'John hit Mary' (NRA) with John swore at Mary (NRSA). In NRSA the narrator's control is even greater than in IS. In DS what the character said (i.e. its propositional content) and how he said it are given. In IS what the character said is reported. In NRSA only the kind of speech act that he used need be indicated. Thus:

The categorization of the presentation of character THOUGHT is essentially the same as that for speech presentation except for one important difference, namely that the norm for thought presentation is not DT but IT, because it is semantically implausible to suggest that we can directly observe the thoughts of others:

This difference is important because it explains the difference in effect obtained when the Free Indirect category is used for speech and thought. Because FIT, in opposition to FIS, is a movement from the norm toward the character end of the continuum, it is perceived by readers as representing closeness with that character, the direct observation of the articulation of his thoughts. It is for this reason that FIS is so commonly used in stream-of-consciousness writing; it apparently allows us to observe a character's unconscious thoughts as they appear.

To interpose an account of speech and thought presentation at this point may seem somewhat laborious. But a knowledge of the categorization of thought presentation is essential to the understanding of the finer workings of Stephen's epiphany. I will now go through the passage indicating changes in the mode of presentation and how they are used, bringing in other stylistic markers to support the analysis. In particular, I will refer to some of the lexical patterning which occurs. For ease of reference I include below a table indicating the patterning of the particular morphemes which I will discuss:

Paragraph	Number of words	Morpheme occurrence*									
		wild	alone	drift	silent	quiet	faint	gentle	soft	life	still
1	88	1	0	5	2	0	0	0	0	0	1
2	51	0	0	0	0	0	0	0	0	0	0
3	63	3	3	0	0	0	0	0	0	1	0
4	140	0	1	0	0	0	0	0	4	0	1
5	102	0	1	0	1	1	4	2	0	0	1
6	11	0	0	0	0	0	0	0	0	0	0
7	56	1	0	0	0	0	0	0	0	1	0
8	96	1	0	0	1	0	0	0	0	4	0

*There are of course many more repetitions in the passage than this table would suggest. This is just a partial analysis of particularly interesting repetitions relative to the interpretative points which I want to make.

We might start by noting that although the whole passage is seen from Stephen's point of view this does not mean that his thoughts are rendered throughout. The first sentence begins with narrative report of the scene in front of Stephen and then moves into NRTA with 'he wondered at the endless drift of seaweed'. The rest of this paragraph consists of narrative report from Stephen's point of view but not a representation of the workings of his mind. We see what Stephen sees, and the scene is located with respect to him by phrases like *above him* and *below him*. The water under his feet and the sky above his head are portrayed in some detail, forming a backdrop with him in the middle. Moreover, there is an obvious internal/external contrast. The sky and water are described in terms which portray them as slow-moving and quiet. The word *drift* occurs twice in the first paragraph, and *drifting* three times. *Silently* occurs twice, we are told that the air is *still*, and Stephen himself moves *slowly*. The verbs of movement (e.g. *swaying, turning*) also suggest slowness. Then, in the last clause Stephen is *described* internally ('a new *wild* life was *singing* in his veins'), where *wild* and *singing* contrast with the suggestions of slow movement and quiet with which the scene has been imbued.

The point about the first paragraph, then, is that it is largely an external description of the scene as we infer Stephen must have witnessed it. Although the workings of his mind are not represented as such. We experience what he experiences. An interesting example of this is the effect of the lack of conjunction reduction at the beginning of sentence 2, 'emerald and black and russet and olive, it moved . . .'. Note that the formation of a list structure in English would normally demand the deletion of the first two *ands*, to produce 'emerald, black, russet and olive . . .'. Joyce's refusal to reduce the conjunctions makes us feel that Stephen views the colours in the seaweed not as one agglomerated whole, but one at a time; first he notices its emerald quality, then its blackness, and so on. Lack of conjunction reduction with similar effects, occurs elsewhere in the passage, in sentences 9 and 10 for instance. Although we see what Stephen sees, because the sentences are in the NRA and NRTA modes they are under the narrator's control; this means that the reader also takes the description to be a reliable one.

The second paragraph, on the other hand, is entirely in FIT and so moves directly into Stephen's mind. All three sentences are questions with third person pronouns and past tense, there is no introductory thinking clause, and the deictic *now* in sentence 5 is appropriate to Stephen's immediate situation. The whole paragraph could possibly be interpreted as direct authorial address to the reader, but we must assume that the omniscient author would have no need to ask such questions, and therefore FIT is the most obvious interpretation. Hence the movement into Stephen's mind at the end of the first paragraph, where his new, wild state of mind is described metaphorically is taken further by the free indirect presentation of his thoughts themselves.

The third paragraph can be seen either as narrative report of Stephen's mental state and position, or alternatively as FIT. Formally, either interpretation would be consistent with the facts. There are no reporting verbs, the tense is past, and the third person pronoun is used. There is considerable lexical repetition and the use of parallel forms both at a syntactic and phonetic level. These choices could be consistent either with a 'poetic' description on the part of the narrator or with an emotionally charged series of character thoughts. The most reasonable explanation, however, would be that sentences 8-10 are FIT, as they appear to be answers to the questions asked in 5-7. Stephen's view is that he is alone (*alone* occurs three times in this paragraph), and yet at the same time he appears to be surrounded by children, girls and their voices. This inconsistency, both in terms of this paragraph and with the description in paragraph 1, where no figures were mentioned, reinforces the suggestion that it is Stephen's thoughts that we are witnessing. This distinction also accounts for another apparent inconsistency, namely that in this paragraph the adjective *wild* is not just predicated of Stephen (as it was in paragraph 1), but also of the air. This conflicts with the description of the scene in the first paragraph with its repetition of *silently* and the phonaesthetic morpheme *drift*. We infer here that Stephen *thinks* that his surroundings are wild because of the mood he is in, whereas we know that they are not because of what the narrator has previously told us.

It should now be becoming clear that the paragraph divisions in this passage coincide with changes in type of presentation. The end of a paragraph does not necessarily mean a change in presentation type, as paragraphs 2 and 3 show; but the type of presentation does not change (as it does in many other novels and at other places in this one) in the middle of a paragraph. This effect of the paragraphing helps the reader notice the conflicts between the narrator's and Stephen's perception of the scene. Paragraphs are also strongly associated with different aspects of the situation. Hence 1 describes the general scene around Stephen, then in 2 Stephen asks questions, which are answered in 3. Paragraph 4 describes what the girl looks like, whereas 5 describes what she does. This use of paragraphs is reflected in the grouping of some of the lexical items. Paragraph 1 contains all five of the occurrences of the morpheme *drift* in the passage and both of the occurrences of *silently* (the morpheme *silent* does occur once each in 5 and 8, but as a noun). *Soft* occurs four times, but only in paragraph 4, and *faint* also occurs four times, but only in paragraph 5, which also contains both of the occurrences of *gently*. *Alone and still* occurs twice, once at the beginning of each of the two paragraphs about the girl. When these points are taken together with the fact that words from common associational groupings tend to go together (see *still, quiet, faint, gently, soft, silence* and *whispering* in 5) it is very apparent that Joyce is using paragraph structure strategically to signal shifts from internal thought to the perception of externals and from one aspect of the description to another.

The fourth paragraph moves us back out of Stephen's mind to a description of the girl he sees in the water. Every sentence in this paragraph begins with a subject noun phrase referring to the girl or some part of her. The description is, however, from Stephen's point of view. This is indicated, for instance, by the locative phrase *before him* and the non-factive verb *seem* in sentence 12. Lexically this paragraph seems consistent with the first (also narrative report from Stephen's point of view). The girl, like the air earlier, is described as *still*; and *soft*, which has associations with *silently* and partial phonetic similarity with *drift*, occurs four times. It is also foregrounded by its occurrence in the balanced repetitive phrase 'soft and slight, slight and soft'.

Paragraph 5 continues the narrative report of 4. The girl is again described in the first sentence of the paragraph as *alone and still*, and the noise which she makes with her foot in the water is described in minimal terms by the repeated use of *faint* and *gently*, verbs like *stirring* and *whispering*, simile ('soft as the bells of sleep') and by the density of onomatopoeically appropriate fricatives and sibilants. The return to the description of the girl's face with 'a faint flame trembled on her cheek' is also consistent with this.

After the soft, external description of the previous two paragraphs, the single sentence of paragraph 6 (which is foregrounded for this reason alone) marks a sudden and extreme shift. We move from very little noise to a lot with the exclamation, *cried* and *outburst*. Moreover, we move from one end of the presentation scale (Narrative Report) to the other with Direct or Free Direct Thought (there are no quotation marks, but it is arguable that the dash is equivalent to them for Joyce). The suddenness of the change is increased by an inversion which places the exclamation next to the narrative report with which it contrasts. Although the use of *cried* and *outburst* at first sight suggests that we are being presented with speech, the fact that *Stephen's soul* is the subject of *cried* indicates that we are witnessing his thoughts. The use of 'noisy' terminology is thus designed to bring out as strongly the soft/loud contrast between the description of the girl and Stephen's reaction. But more importantly, this, along with all the other features which make the single sentence of paragraph 6 stand out, indicates that this is the sudden moment of change and realization which characterizes the epiphany. The fact that DT and FDT are structurally like soliloquy also gives the impression that the realization marked by the exclamation is a conscious one.

Paragraph 7 returns to Narrative Report from Stephen's point of view. But now it describes *him*, and so is emotionally highly charged. It contains literally untrue statements which are metaphors for strong emotions ('cheeks were aflame', 'body was aglow'), loud utterance words (*crying, singing*), the word *wildly*, which links with paragraph 3, and the heavy repetition of 'on and on and on and on'. In the last paragraph this highly charged description gives way to the interior portrayal of emotional thoughts. Except for sentences 27 and 29 (which because of their verbless, exclamatory nature are perhaps best treated as FDT) the paragraph is in FIT. Stephen's highly individual perception of events is marked by statements made to himself which the reader must take as untrue. It is hard to interpret the fact that the girl looked at him because she felt his eyes on her as a 'call', and she was certainly not a wild angel, as Stephen appears to assume. The portrayal here is consistent with the individual view of paragraphs 3 and 7, and the linking of emotional involvement ('on and on and on and on') with sin ('to err, to fall') helps explain why Stephen's original outburst of joy was *profane*. That he has decided to throw over religion for life and beauty together can be seen in the description of the wild angel as 'the angel of mortal youth and beauty'.

We have passed briefly over many aspects of this passage (e.g. phonetic patterning and lexical repetition), and ignored others altogether (e.g. the passage's 'poetic' quality and the lexical items associated with religion). But it should now be clear why it is an 'epiphany' passage and why it marks Stephen's rejection of religion for life and beauty. I hope that the reader will also understand more clearly how Joyce strategically manipulates variation in the mode of presentation of Stephen's thoughts and perceptions in conjunction with lexical repetition and paragraph structuring to achieve the climactic outburst which characterizes the end of the passage.

Conclusion

There have been many attempts by linguists to suggest that stylistic analysis can be of help to literary studies, but on the whole these suggestions have not been taken up by the critics. I have tried to take the linguists' case a step further by arguing for the centrality of stylistic analysis within the core concerns of criticism. More importantly, I hope to have demonstrated this by an, albeit partial, explicit analysis as well as by general argument. This explicit link between linguistic structure and meaning and effect is, I would claim, also crucial for the *teaching* of literature, particularly to those students who do not already possess the sensitivity to respond in a precise enough way to literature. For it is only via such explicit linking that the understanding of how literature works can be achieved, either for the native student of English or for the student from overseas.

References

1. I assume as a conventional starting point the publication of R. Fowler, (ed.), *Essays on Style and Language*, London; Routledge, 1966.
2. See, for example Paul Werth's demonstration (in 'Roman Jakobson's Verbal Analysis of Poetry,' *Journal of Linguistics*, 12, No. 1, 1976, pp.21–73) that a Shakespearean sonnet, a poem by William MacGonagall and a Leader from *The Times* all exhibited the same amount of patterning.
3. 'How Ordinary is Ordinary Language?', *New Literary History*, 5, No. 1, 1973, pp.41–54.
4. *Toward a Speech Act Theory of Literary Discourse*, Indiana; Indiana U.P., 1977, chapter 1.
5. For a complete analysis of this poem, along with a number of others, in the context of a study empirically validating the notion of foregrounding, see Willy Van Peer, *The Stylistic Theory of Foregrounding: A Theoretical and Empirical Investigation*, unpublished Ph.D. thesis, University of Lancaster, 1980.
6. For an informative account of parallelism see G. N. Leech, *A Linguistic Guide to English Poetry*, London; Longman, 1969, pp.62–9.
7. For a brief explanation of speech act theory see J. Searle, 'What is a Speech Act' in P. P. Giglioli (ed.), *Language and Social Context*, Harmondsworth; Penguin, 1975, pp.136–54.
8. For an introductory account of foregrounding see Leech, 1969, *op. cit.*, chapter 4.
9. For a work which explores the role of language as a social conditioner see R. Fowler *et al.*, *Language and Control*, London; Routledge, 1979.
10. T. Connolly (ed.), *Joyce's PORTRAIT*, London; Peter Owen, 1964.
11. For a good example of literary practical criticism see Ian Watt, 'The First Paragraph of *The Ambassadors*', *Essays in Criticism*, 10, 1960, pp.250–74.
12. The reader may well object that this piece of prose is a particularly poetic example. Though this is true, it should become apparent that the points which I want to make do not relate to the 'poeticality' of the passage.

13. 'Art and *A Portrait of the Artist*' in Connolly, *op. cit.*, pp.156–67.
14. *James Joyce*, New York; O.U.P., 1959, p.151.
15. 'The Calling of Stephen Dedalus' in Connolly, *op. cit.*, pp.114–24.
16. London; Longman, 1981.
17. For a good recent survey see B. McHale, 'Free Indirect Discourse; a Survey of Recent Accounts', *Poetics and Theory of Literature*, 3, 1978, pp.235–87.

STRESS, RHYTHM AND INTONATION IN THE STUDY OF ENGLISH LITERATURE

Susan Ramsaran
University College, London

Introduction

English literature emanates from a culture that has not maintained a rich oral tradition. Because of this perhaps we tend to forget that speech is the primary form of language and that writing has evolved as a means of conveying speech to large numbers of people and over great distances. Of course written literature has developed a great many conventions of its own. But it is worth remembering that drama is designed for oral delivery, that the sound of speech is implicit in poetry and that a clear prose writer chooses his language in such a way as to make it unambiguous when it is read aloud. An orthodox literary analysis of poetic technique takes into account such obvious features as alliteration and rhyme; but there are other aspects of the sound of speech which are surely important for a full appreciation of literature.

One major area where little work has been done is in the relationship between the stress, rhythm and intonation of literature and of everyday speech. To some extent this matter touches on poetic metre, but it has wider relevance to literature in general and is in some ways more complex.

1. Stress and Rhythm

Stress and rhythm are inseparable (when one looks at stretches of speech that are longer than a word or two) since, in the case of English, rhythm is the patterning of stresses in the language. However, it is possible to look specifically at the placement of a particular stress and at the effect of this on the pronunciation of a particular word. This section, then, will discuss both the rhythmic patterning of a combination of stresses and the effects of the occurrence of an individual stress.

The fact that English has stress-timed rhythm means that the stresses tend to occur at roughly equal intervals in time. This regularity is most apparent over short stretches of speech, rhythmic groups which correspond to the intonation groups which are variously called tone units, sense groups or word groups in various terminologies.[1] Generally it happens that there are different numbers of syllables between each pair of stresses with the result that a sequence of four unstressed syllables, for instance, will be hurried over more quickly than another group of, say, two unstressed syllables in the same tone unit. Thus /ˈsɔvrənti ðət/ will take up about the same length of time as /ˈhiːdz bət/ in

'Death with a 'sovereignty that 'heeds but 'hides . . .
(from *The Wreck of the Deutschland*, XXXII, by Hopkins)

This example of speech rhythm is deliberately chosen from a Hopkins poem, as this is the essence of Hopkins' 'sprung rhythm'. It is like the natural speech rhythm of English, unlike most metrical verse in which constant numbers of unstressed syllables occur between the stresses. Hopkins imposes a strict rhythmic structure on his verse by controlling the number of stresses. So, for example, in *The Wreck of the Deutschland*, the fourth line of nearly every stanza has three stresses but the syllables vary from four to twelve, just as the rapidity with which unstressed syllables are uttered varies in normal spoken English. The corresponding line from each of four stanzas will serve to illustrate this:

I 'whirled out 'wings that 'spell	(III)
And it 'crowds and it 'combs to the 'fall	(IV)
'Swings the 'stroke 'dealt	(VI)
The 'girth of it and the 'wharf of it and the 'wall	(XXXII)

Finally in this poem, when Hopkins has firmly established his approach to rhythm, he forces us to read the very end of the poem with a stress on eight out of ten words:

Our 'heart's 'charity's 'hearth's 'fire, our 'thoughts' 'chivalry's 'throng's 'Lord.   (XXXV)

Every content word here is stressed, and since the majority of them are monosyllabic, the poem concludes with a great emphatic weight of adjacent stresses.

Another poet who makes use of natural speech rhythms, but with quite different effect, is John Betjeman. Perhaps it would be helpful to look at an extract from an amusing satirical poem with the main stresses marked on it:

You 'ask me what it is I 'do. Well 'actually, you 'know,
I'm 'partly a li'aison man and 'partly P.R.'O.
Es'sentially I 'integrate the 'current export 'drive
And 'basically I'm 'viable from 'ten o'clock till 'five.

For 'vital off-the-'record work — that's 'talking transport-'wise —
I've a 'scarlet Aston-'Martin — and 'does she go? She 'flies!
[from *Executive* by Betjeman]

The many unstressed syllables give an impression of a very fast pace which is particularly appropriate to the 'life-style' of the subject of the poem. The concentration of imprecise fashionable expressions gently satirizes the get-ahead bombastic young executives who use them, whilst the regularity of the swift rhythm contributes to the impression of slickness. The metre does not deviate from a perfectly possible conversational rhythm: form words and content words are spaced so as to make stresses fall at regular intervals in time on the content words. But — and this is the artificial regularity — with only two exceptions there are exactly four syllables between every pair of stresses and every line is end-stopped on a stressed (rhyming) monosyllable. This balance of naturalness and contrivance adds to the reader's amusement.

The comic use of rhythmic devices is something which it may be difficult for the foreign speaker of English to appreciate. When it occurs in combination with some other linguistic joke, it is easier to interpret the 'tone'[2] of the poem. For instance, everyone knows Keats' *Ode on a Grecian Urn* and so they immediately recognize Desmond Skirrow's affectionately mocking intention in his *Ode on a Grecian Urn summarized*:

> Gods chase
> Round vase.
> What say?
> What play?
> Don't know.
> Nice, though.

Skirrow trivializes Keats' philosophical questioning by simplifying the questions along with the syntax. The total omission of form words leaves us with telegram-like sentences and we find ourselves putting stresses on every single word of the poem. This very *un*naturalness of rhythm (in contrast to Betjeman's apparent naturalness) is a clue to the comic intent of the poet.

Other types of unnaturalness are the regular jogging metres of alternate stressed and unstressed syllables and the light, ballad-like metres where all lines have identical rhythms, an example of the latter kind being

> The 'sight of the 'English is 'getting me 'down.
> Fly 'westward, my 'heart, from this 'festering 'town . . .
> (from *Hiraeth in N.W.3.* by Wynford Vaughan-Thomas)

In a case like this, rhyme on the stressed final monosyllables makes the regularity of the rhythm more obtrusive. Perhaps the native speaker's subjective reaction to such tidy patterning is to find it glib, and so the comic effect is heightened.

This interplay of rhyme and rhythm is particularly apparent in the case of feminine rhyme, a marked example of this being the feminine rhyme across word boundaries in

> This piteous news so much it shocked her,
> She quite forgot to send the Doctor,
> To comfort poor old Susan Gale.
> (from *The Idiot Boy* by Wordsworth)

Doctor has to be pronounced ('dɒkte/ and Wordsworth's insistence on rhyme in this poem reminds us to read *shocked her* as /'ʃɔkt ə/. /ə/ is a perfectly normal weak form of *her* and is the one which we would expect in an unstressed position like this. It is clearly important to get the pronunciation right as the heroic couplets and the potentially tragic theme lead us to expect a serious poem. But the trivializing effect of rhythmic devices (amongst others) indicates that *The Idiot Boy* is, in fact, mock heroic.

A knowledge of the relationship between stress and weak forms is also important for an effective reading of another humorous poem, Ted Pauker's *A Grouchy Good Night to the Academic Year.* The poem has a light, wryly satirical 'tone' although it makes some telling points. This tolerant good humour is partly conveyed by weak forms included in feminine rhymes, such as

> Good night to the Session — portentous   /pɔ'tentəs/
> Inside the Vice-Chancellor's gown,
> The personage who'll represent us   /repri'zent əs/
> To Public and Party and Crown.

In this poem it is important to use the normal weak forms of everyday English, for instance /əs/ rather than /ʌs/. These are always unstressed whereas strong forms are usually stressed — and if the stress falls on a form word because of the metre, that word must have its strong form. Hence once Betjeman has established a very regular rhythm in his poem *In Westminster Abbey* we find that we are forced by the rhythm to put stresses on certain form words, for instance on *as, and* and *to* in the first stanza:

> 'Let me 'take this 'other 'glove off
> 'As the 'vox hu'mana 'swells
> 'And the 'beauteous 'fields of 'Eden
> 'Bask be'neath the 'Abbey 'bells.
> 'Here, where 'England's 'statesmen 'lie,
> 'Listen 'to a 'lady's 'cry.

This device seems to be partly responsible for indicating that the 'tone' is ironic. The native speaker of English feels that although the whole poem is in the first person, the poet does not intend us to take it at its face value, that in fact he is satirizing the attitude expressed here. Irony is something which it is extremely difficult for the foreigner to recognize. A straight lyrical poem is perhaps the easiest type to understand but how is he to know when a poem is not saying what it seems to be saying? It seems likely that rhythmic distortions like those mentioned here (in conjunction with incongruous lexical juxtapositions) may provide a clue that irony is intended.

In case the reader is doubtful about this, a little supporting evidence is provided by P. G. Wodehouse who deliberately italicizes *from*, indicating that the stress is to fall on a form word, thus converting it from its expected pronunciation /frəm/ to its strong form /'frɔm/ to contribute to a rhyme across three words with *tomahawk*:

> Then, as a pigeon attempts to fly *from* a hawk,
> Hastily winging its way through the blue,
> So did the reveller, dropping his tomahawk,
> Flee at the sight, Colonel CODY, of you.
>
> (from *To William (Whom We Have Missed)* by P. G. Wodehouse)

Writing satirically, Pope requires that we should be aware of the normal weak forms in a couplet like the following:

> Wit shoots in vain its momentary fires,
> The meteor drops, and in a flash expires.
>
> (from *The Dunciad* (iv. 653-4) by Pope)

Here the metaphor is sustained through the couplet, the rhyme words *fires* and *expires* point the contrast, and the rhythm of *and in a flash* with its quick unstressed words /ənd in ə 'flæ ʃ/ supports the meaning of the phrase within the couplet which contributes to the meaning of the whole.

It is always important to remember that English uses stress contrastively. Very rarely does it actually distinguish between pairs of words (as in *billow* /'biləu/ and *below* /bi'ləu/), but it frequently marks a contrast in conversation as in an utterance like This present isn't *from* /'frɔm/ my mother: it's *for* /'fɔ:/ my mother

Sometimes a poet takes care to indicate the placing of such stresses, as Pope does by means of capital letters in

> Hope springs eternal in the human breast.
> Man never Is, but always To be blest.
>
> (from *An Essay on Man* (1. 95-6) by Pope)

The stress placement is thus largely responsible for conveying the important and serious contrast between man's *present* misfortunes and his optimism about the *future*.

2. Contrast and Nuclear Tone

It will be noticed that at the end of the section on stress and rhythm, the example illustrating contrastive stress requires pitch change also. The reference of certain words, such as *only*, is made clear in spoken English by the placement of the intonational nucleus (the syllable in the tone unit which carries the major stress and pitch change). Perhaps this is most clearly illustrated by three utterances where the pitch is high on the stressed syllable marked ['] and low on succeeding syllables. Thus

<pre>
I 'only °grow `vegetables   (not flowers)
I 'only `grow °vegetables   (I don't eat them)
I only °grow °vegetables   (I don't do anything else)
</pre>

In writing, such distinctions are generally conveyed by careful word ordering; but in poetry with a strict metre, the verse rhythm indicates where the stresses should occur and the poet relies on the reader to locate the nucleus appropriately by initiating the pitch change on the right word. For instance `Love could conceivably be the nucleus in the next extract; but because of the demands of the metre, it would seem most suitable to stress *Love* and begin the nuclear fall from *only*, following it with a slight pause as shown below. (The other intonation marks represent just one possible version.)

<pre>
My ˅form,/ my ,friends ob°serve with ,pain,/
    Is 'growing °daily `thinner./
'Love `only/ 'occupies the °brain
    That °once could °think of `dinner./
</pre>

(from *The Gourmet's Love Song* by P. G. Wodehouse)

The discussion up to this point has concentrated on comic and ironic verse, as it is particularly difficult for the foreigner to recognize the 'tone' of such verse. A study of the rhythm of spoken English may well help him to detect the poet's ironic or comic intentions since exaggerated adherence to the rules of speech rhythms or, alternatively, deviation from them, provide the clues. The correct placement of the intonational nucleus is essential for the sympathetic reading of any literature as the following examples will show.

In Chaucer's *Knight's Tale* Palamon says

<pre>
And now thou wouldest falsely been about
To love my lady, whom I love and serve[3] (1142–3)
</pre>

The reader must resist the temptation to put the nucleus in the unmarked (likely or normally expected) position at the end of the line. Nor may he break the rule of English nuclear placement to put it on *love* which is 'given' (as opposed to new) information or, at least, lexical repetition — and such words cannot provide the nucleus. Instead, it is appropriately placed on *I*, indignantly contrasting the usurper Arcite with the speaker who has a prior claim to the lady's love, the claim of longstanding fidelity.

Occasionally nuclear placement is affected by the syntactic function of a particular word. For instance we do not usually expect to locate it on the auxiliary verb *will*. However, *will* is the nucleus in

<pre>
I wish I didn't talk so much at parties.
When hotly boil the arguments,
Ah! would I had the common sense
To sit demurely on a fence
    And let who `will be vocal . . .
</pre>

(from *Reflections at Dawn* by Phyllis McGinley)

Here *will* is not the auxiliary conveying the future tense. It is the main verb indicating volition: 'And let anyone be vocal who *wants* to be vocal.' If we fail to read *will* as the nucleus, it is impossible to make sense of the sentence.

Correct nuclear placement is just as important for the understanding of prose as it is in reading poetry. It is, of course, of the utmost importance when reading conversational passages which are supposed to represent specific utterances of spoken English. The following exchange comes from *The Years* by Virginia Woolf: Peggy says to Martin

'I was wondering how they came to marry', she said. 'Were they in love?' She spoke at random to distract him.
'Of course he was in love,' he said. He looked at Delia. She was standing by the fireplace

After half a page of further conversation, Peggy resumes

'But Delia —' she asked; Delia was passing them. 'Was she in love?'

The reader may at first be somewhat puzzled by the partial repetition of Peggy's question. But Virginia Woolf has provided the clues for those who are familiar with English intonation: the neutral way of asking her first question would be

'Were they in ˌlove? (with *love* starting at a low pitch and rising)

We expect an answer which takes the form *Yes* or *No* or some elaborate conversational substitute for one of these. *Of ˈcourse* would be an emphatic substitute for *Yes* but this would require a repetition of *they were in love* following the nucleus. Instead Martin says '*he* was in love' and the nuclear placement has to be on *he*, since it cannot occur on the repeated item *in love* and its location on *course* would be incompatible with the unexpected word *he* following. Hence the reader is left (as is Peggy) in puzzled suspense until an opportunity to ask a further question with contrastive, searching nuclear placement on *she*:

Was she in °love?

Marked nuclear placement is often necessary if we are to place contrasts where the poet intends them to occur. After the statement 'It wasn't a dream', if we want to suggest the possibility that it *was* in fact a dream, we will have to emphasize *was* by making it the nucleus. Thus the most straightforward reading of the following lines involves a falling and then rising of the pitch on *was* as indicated below:

It was no dream; or say a dream it ˇwas,
Real are the dreams of Gods, and smoothly pass
Their pleasures in a long imˋmortal dream.
(from *Lamia* by Keats)

It seems most likely that the nucleus of the last tone unit will fall in *immortal*, focusing attention on the kind of dream that it must have been.

In addition to placing the nucleus appropriately, the reader has to choose a suitable nuclear tone. The 'straightforward' reading suggested above has a fall-rise nuclear tone on *was* which implies both a contradiction of the preceding statement and an indication that a qualification is to follow. Other nuclear tones are always possible and, in fact, it is often the varying of nuclear tones which is responsible for conveying widely different interpretations of the same words.

Different interpretations of Shakespeare often depend on the use of different nuclear tones and it becomes apparent that the variations are numerous when we see how even the most simple utterances can be subtly changed by intonation.

The opening scene of *Romeo and Juliet*, for instance, contains a quarrel between servants of the two rival households. In the text the dialogue is shown baldly as

> *Samson* (a Capulet): I serve as good a man as you
> *Abraham* (a Montague): No better
> *Samson*: Well sir
> *Gregory* (a Capulet): Say better: here comes one of my master's kinsmen.

Abraham's two words can be uttered as a firm, loyal statement with a fall on *better*. But, to suggest just one plausible alternative, it can be said with a low, threatening rise on *better*, taunting Samson and challenging him to a duel. That one use of a marked nuclear tone which changes a syntactic statement into a question can characterize Abraham as a belligerent servant eager to goad Samson into a fight. This interpretation of Abraham's words would reveal that even the servants are keen to continue and intensify the feud. Thus the hopelessness of the lovers' passion for each other is emphasized early on in the play, even before the entrance of any major character. Again, if a minor character's utterance can be varied so significantly in terms of its intonation, how much more importantly and complexly must this apply to the speeches of the major characters.

The poetry of a major soliloquy offers immense scope for variation, but we can glimpse the possibilities by merely examining another short exchange, this time one between King Lear and Cordelia:

> *Lear*: So young, and so untender?
> *Cordelia*: So young, my lord, and true. (I.i. 108–9)

There is space here to discuss only two versions of each of these speeches, Briefly, Lear could stress *young* on a fairly low pitch and then have a nuclear tone beginning to rise from low pitch on *tender*:

So, ˌyoung and so unˌtender?

This sounds like an angry, querying demand for an explanation from his daughter. If, on the other hand, *young* were fairly high pitched and the following syllables were each successively lower until a fall-rise nuclear tone, the effect would be one of a far more puzzled, desolate sort of question:

So ˎyoung and °so unˇtender?

Cordelia could echo this pattern, expressing a gently contradictory statement:

So ˎyoung my °lord and ˇtrue.

Alternatively she could keep *my lord and* on the same fairly high pitch as *young* and then drop down for a fall which begins fairly low on *true*:

So 'young my °lord and ˌtrue.

In this case she would convey serious, heartfelt sincerity in her incontrovertible statement.

These two comparatively simple examples show to what a great extent characterization is dependent on intonation. The example from *King Lear* also reminds us of the way that attention is focused on new information by the location of the nucleus. A simple fall could not occur on *young* as that is a repeated item. It is worth noticing the effect of an exchange like

A I 'thought you were °young andˋinnocent.
B I 'told you I'm °young and ˋinnocent.

The effect of placing the nucleus on a repeated word is incongruous: we expect some final contrasting adjective when we hear the preparatory parallelism of intonation and content, such as

I 'told you I'm °young but exˋperienced.

The fact that the information focus turns out to emphasize rather than refute A's statement may be used to achieve a mischievously witty anticlimax. In Cordelia's speech *young could* be the nucleus if a fall-rise nuclear tone were used, as this would imply 'Young, yes; but what is more important, true'.

We see how important it is that the reader appreciates the different conversational implications of various nuclear tones when we look at the beginning of a poem like this:

Evans? Yes, many a time
I came down his bare flight
Of stairs into the gaunt kitchen
(from *Evans* by R. S. Thomas)

It sounds as if we have come in the middle of a conversation and the reader has to decide whether to read the first word with the high rise nuclear tone of a casual question or perhaps with a more searching fall-rise. (ˊEvans? Is that who you mean? ˏWell . . .)

Some lines from the poetry of *Winnie the Pooh* provide a particularly good illustration of the way in which variations in nuclear tone convey different implications:

> Three cheers for Pooh!
> (*For who*?)
> For Pooh —
> (*Why what did he do*?)
> I thought you knew;
> He saved his friend from a wetting! . . .
> Well, Pooh was a Bear of Enormous Brain . . .
> But he managed to float
> On a sort of boat
> (*On a sort of what*?)
> Well, a sort of pot —
>
> (from *Anxious Pooh Song* by A. A. Milne)

The regularity of the rhyme forces the reader to put the intonational nuclei on appropriate words. He can then vary the nuclear tones at will—and by doing this, the student of English can experiment with the way in which different attitudes are conveyed by various intonation patterns. A high rise in the question *For ˈwho*? would be suitable for a casual query; whilst a high unstressed prehead followed by a low rise ˉFor ˏwho? could indicate incredulous amazement that Pooh of all people should deserve three cheers. (The rhyme is also a reminder of the normal conversational form *who*.) Similarly, the two occurrences of *well* invite the reader to use different intonation patterns: in 'Well, Pooh was a Bear of Enormous Brain' the *well* is a conversational introductory word, probably unstressed and low pitched; but in 'On a sort of what? Well, a sort of pot', one might read ˋwell with a firm high fall preceding the explanation or ˇwell with an apologetic self-correcting fall-rise.

Most of the examples in this section have presented the reader with a choice to make: his decision about which nuclear tone to use influences his interpretation of the text. Sometimes, however, the reader has little choice; but he has to make the right decision in order to read the text sympathetically and appreciate its implications.

For instance, in the couplet:

> All this dread ORDER break — for whom? for thee?
> Vile worm? — oh Madness, Pride, Impiety!
>
> (from *An Essay on Man* (I. 257–8) by Pope)

Overgeneralizations are sometimes made about the use of different nuclear tones. Questions can be asked on rises or on falls. The straightforward version of a *wh-* question has a fall. Here, then, the neutral reading of *for* `*whom* has a fall. A fall cannot, however, occur on a question which has the syntax of a statement: it is the rise on *for   thee* which turns the phrase into a question. It will be noticed, then, that the syntactic form of these two questions dictates that there will be a variety of nuclear tones and the attitude conveyed is one of abrupt disapproval and then of scathing doubt, an appropriate implication preceding the exclamatory *vile worm!*.

Earlier it was suggested that rhythm might indicate that a certain poem is to be taken ironically. When other linguistic clues point to a writer's ironic intent, a reader should be aware of any nuclear tone that he can use that might be particularly appropriate to irony, for instance the rise-fall in *Woman's Constancy* by Donne which begins:

> Now thou hast lov'd me one whole day,
> Tomorrow when thou leav'st, what wilt thou say?

A constancy which lasts no longer than a day (even if a whole day!) is inconstancy. The note of defiant complaint in the poet's voice may be suggested by avoiding a simple fall at the end and instead reading it as:

> For by tomorrow, `I may °think so ^too.

A prose passage which exemplifies the importance of making a correct choice of nuclear tone comes from *Jane Eyre* by Charlotte Brontë at the point where Rochester is concealing from Jane the fact that he is already married. Her response to his deceitful mention of some minor obstacle to their marrying is:

> 'Is that all! Thank God it is no worse!'

A firm fall on *that* would suit the exclamation here, whereas a rise (Is ˏthat all) would immediately convey an unsuitably doubtful query indicating lack of trust; and a rise on *all* ('Is that ˏall) could be a cheerful question, even a question whose implication is a hope that there is more.

In Middlemarch by George Eliot, Will Ladislaw says of Dorothea:

> 'I never had a *preference* for her, any more than I have a preference for breathing.'

It is interesting to compare this with Catherine's statement about Heathcliff in *Wuthering Heights* by Emily Brontë ('I *am* Heathcliff' and the fact that her love for him 'resembles the eternal rocks beneath: a source of little visible delight, but necessary'). In other words, the lover feels a sense of identity with the beloved and the concept of *preference* is a ridiculously irrelevant one. The way to convey the unsuitability of the word is probably to use a fall-rise on it, the implication of that tone being 'not *that* word: you *must* use a more appropriate one'.

In the Scott Montcrieff translation of Proust's *A la Recherche du Temps Perdu* comes a passage in which the narrator closes his mind to disillusionment as, having penetrated fashionable society, he tries to ignore his suspicion that, despite its exclusiveness, it has entertainments no more extraordinary than those of his own class:

> Was it really for the sake of dinners such as this that all these people dressed themselves up and refused to allow the penetration of middle-class women into their so-exclusive drawing rooms—for dinners such as this? The same, had I been absent? The suspicion flashed across my mind for a moment, but it was too absurd. Plain commonsense enabled me to brush it aside.

(*The Guermantes Way* Pt II Vol VI)

The ironical 'tone' here needs to be enhanced by suitable intonation and the narrator's naïvety may be expressed by, for instance, an incredulous high head and low rise on the repetition of *for 'dinners such as ,this.*

The incongruous effect of the wrong choice of intonation may be illustrated by the use of this same pattern on the famous line from Marlowe's *Doctor Faustus*:

> 'Was ,this the °face that °launched a °thousand °ships?

The critical incredulity implied by this pattern ruins what is supposed to be a hushed exclamation of wonder, wonder which might even be best conveyed by a level nuclear tone on *ships* so that this tone unit is closely linked to the next.

3. Tone Unit Boundaries

Marlowe's verse provides some material for a fruitful study of the boundaries between tone units. He appears to be somewhat influenced by the tradition of mid-line caesuras, a typical example being:

> Why this is hell: nor am I out of it.

(*Doctor Faustus*)

Even in less extreme cases, his lines show a tendency to have a break in this position, perhaps simply offering the reader an opportunity to start a fresh tone unit at that point even if he does not choose to realize the potential pause. For instance:

> Be ˅thou on ˅earth/ as 'Jove is in the ˋsky,/

would seem a perfectly possible reading. When a break is clearly located elsewhere, therefore, it can have marked significance. For example an early caesura after *O* could suggest a gasp followed by a rapid rush of breathless admiration after the moment of inspiration in the lines:

> `O/ thou art 'fairer than the °evening °air,
> °Clad in the °beauty of a °thousand stars/

(*Doctor Faustus*)

This is, of course, not the only way to read these lines but it does illustrate how a sensitive use of English intonation patterns can contribute to an effective interpretation of the verse.

Generally we might expect that the tone unit boundaries will coincide with the ends of lines. Poets can exploit these expectations as does William Carlos Williams in:

> Why bother where I went?
> For I went spinning on the
>
> four wheels of my car
> along the wet road until
>
> I saw a girl with one leg
> over the rail of a balcony

Because the second and fourth lines are not syntactically complete, we run on past the line endings looking for a tone unit boundary. But the penultimate line could be syntactically complete and we are lured into locating the nucleus of that group on `*leg* and making a break for the end of that tone unit at the line's end. Only after the shock of doing so, do we realize that the bathetic prepositional phrase that follows belongs to the same group and that the nucleus should come on *balcony* rather than *leg*.

If end-stopped lines imply tone unit boundaries (but not necessarily pauses) then *enjambement* can be used by a poet for special effect, as Keats uses it in *Calidore*:

> The bowery shore
> Went off in gentle windings to the hoar
> And light blue mountains . . .

The prolongation of the tone unit despite the intervening line ends conveys the gently flowing motion of the boat as Calidore rows peacefully on the lake.

In contrast, Pope uses variation in rhythm (specifically achieved by marked positioning of tone unit boundaries) for dramatic effect:

> See! from the Brake the whirring Pheasant springs,
> And mounts exulting on triumphant Wings!
> Short is his Joy! He feels the fiery Wound

(from *Windsor-Forest* (111–13) by Pope)

Here again, after the initial exclamatory pause, the line gathers momentum as the unbroken phrase moves towards a climax. Then, after the swift movement of the first two lines comes a sharp statement of foreboding monosyllables: 'short is his joy' — as is the tone unit in sudden contrast to the preceding one. From then Pope can turn the horrified reader to a hostility against man's wanton destructiveness.

Sometimes rhythmic variation is less obvious and is not clearly connected with metre. An interesting passage is to be found in Milton's *Comus* when the unruly rout are dancing riotously before the entry of the lady Virtue:

> Come, let us our rites begin;
> 'Tis only daylight that makes sin,
> Which these dun shades will ne'er report.
> Hail, goddess of nocturnal sport . . .
> Come, knit hands, and beat the ground,
> In a light fantastic round.
> Break off, break off, I feel the different pace
> Of some chaste footing near about this ground. (125–8; 143–6)

The native speaker of English may feel intuitively that the rhythm changes significantly at 'Break off' but it is almost impossible to demonstrate this by a conventional metrical analysis. Only three of the eight lines quoted (the first, fifth and sixth) share a regular trochaic metre. Since lines 2, 3 and 4 are all metrically different, there would not seem to be a firmly enough established rhythm for line 7 to stand out as departing from it. Moreover, a simple analysis shows that lines 3 and 7 share the same iambic metre and so, despite its extra foot, the rhythm of line 7 should not contrast so sharply with that of the preceding lines as to make us feel a new rhythmic start.

The explanation, I suggest, is to be found in the division into tone units. Tone unit boundaries come at the ends of each of lines 1 – 6. The only definite line-internal boundaries come after the single monosyllabic nuclear words *Come, Hail* and *Come* at the beginnings of lines 1, 4 and 5 respectively. (There is one other possible boundary after 'knit hands' in line 5 but this is by no means certain.) At line 7, however, there are two definite line-internal boundaries and the strong possibility of having no boundary at the end of the run-on line. It is, in addition, plausible that another line-internal boundary should occur in line 8. Thus, after six lines which each comprise from six to eight syllables in a single tone unit, the boundary of each of which coincides with the line ending, we have:

> Break `off/ break `off/ I 'feel the 'different 'pace
> Of 'some 'chaste `footing/ near a͜bout this ˌground/

This reading is reasonably well supported by the punctuation which is surely meant to imply intonational features. Certainly punctuation does so in *Paradise Lost* where there is great variation of pace in the battle scene of

Book VI. This is partly achieved by the varying length of the tone units and the different locations of their boundaries in relation to the line endings. From the leisurely majesty of blank verse with elaborately complex syntax, Milton moves to using short, unconnected sentences to convey the fast-moving desperation as the battle rages:

> . . . no thought of flight,
> None of retreat, no unbecoming deed
> That argued fear; each on himself relied,
> As only in his arm the moment lay
> Of victory; deeds of eternal fame
> Were done, but infinite; for wide was spread
> That war and various; sometimes on firm ground
> A standing fight, then soaring on main wing
> Tormented all the air; all air seemed then
> Conflicting fire. (VI, 236–45)

Here the irregular placement of tone unit boundaries in relation to line endings, causes a tension which contributes a sense of conflict.

A different effect is achieved by another seventeenth-century poet who also uses variations of rhythmic groupings to enhance his subject matter. The varying length of the lines in Vaughan's *The Water-fall* suggests visually what the varying length of the tone units does even more dramatically: they imitate the tumbling rush of the waterfall as compared with the smooth-flowing stream, and the pace is increased by the marked rhyme scheme. At the same time the quick movement of the waterfall is contrasted with the leisurely movement of the patterned subject of his contemplation and with his swelling confidence. As the lines and the tone units are not commensurate, the suggested boundaries of the latter are marked in the quotation below:

> With what deep murmurs through times silent stealth/
> Doth thy transparent, cool and watery wealth
>   Here flowing fall,/
>   And chide,/ and call,/
> As if his liquid, loose Retinue staid
> Lingring,/ and were of this steep place afraid,/
>   The common pass/
>   Where,/ clear as glass,/
>   All must descend/
>   Not to an end:/
> But quickened by this deep and rocky grave,/
> Rise to a longer course more bright and brave./

Although this discussion has concentrated on poetry, the placement of tone unit boundaries applies as much to prose as to verse. In fact, the second sentence of this article illustrates an ambiguity in this matter: does *perhaps* refer to 'because of this' or to 'we tend to forget'? If the boundary follows *this*, Be'cause of ˅this/ per'haps we °tend to for°get . . ., it is not certain that we forget. But if we do so, the reason is assumed to be clear. However, if the boundary comes between *perhaps* and *we*, Be˅cause of ˅this per°haps/ we 'tend to for°get . . ., our forgetting is certain but the reason is only tentatively suggested. Good writing does not contain many ambiguities like this in matters of fact.

4.   The Contribution of Phonetics

This leads to the final point that a knowledge of the stress, rhythm and intonation of normal spoken English can be of considerable help in evaluating literary texts. For instance, one or two of Keats's early poems show a certain ineptness in his handling of rhythm. *I stood tip-toe*, a slight poem, has such an emphatically regular rhythm that one finds oneself thrown off balance when it changes and almost forces one to put an incorrect stress on the second syllable of *primroses*:

> What next? A tuft of evening primroses,
> O'er which the mind may hover till it dozes;

On Receiving a Curious Shell and a Copy of Verses has a strained metre and contrived rhyme. Word order and diction are forced by the verse form, for instance:

> That goblet right heavy, and massy, and gold.

An example of unpolished prose writing is to be found, surprisingly, in Virginia Woolf where someone at a party in *The Years* breaks a glass and the hostess comes up:

> 'That's the thirteenth glass broken tonight!' said Delia, coming up and stopping in front of them. 'But don't mind—don't mind. They're very cheap—glasses.'

Does the dash before *glasses* represent a pause of hesitation? If so, is it because the hostess is distracted by something else? In that case we simply read a pause into *They're 'very ˅cheap glasses*. Or is it a pause of resentment? Should we then read *They're ˎvery cheap ˎglasses*? Or does she mean 'Glasses are very cheap things'? This would lead to the version *They're 'very ˅cheap ˎglasses*. This uncertainty on the part of the reader simply makes the passage difficult to understand and adds nothing to characterization or to the drama of the situation. Instead we are left with an irritatingly unresolved ambiguity.

On the other hand, in richly-textured poetic writing (whether prose or verse), ambiguity often makes a positive contribution. Therefore the greater the reader's knowledge of the stress, rhythm and intonation of speech, the greater can be his awareness of potential variation in interpretation, and ultimately the greater his appreciation and enjoyment of the literature.

References

The analysis of intonation here follows the system expounded in O'Connor, J. D. and Arnold, G. F., *Intonation of Colloquial English* (2nd ed. 1973), London: Longman.
Armstrong, L. E. and Ward, I. C., (1926), *Handbook of English Intonation*, Leipzig and Berlin: Teubner; (1931) Cambridge: Heffer.
Crystal, D., *Prosodic Systems and Intonation in English*, (1969), Cambridge: CUP.

Notes

1. 'tone unit' by Crystal (1969), 'sense group' by Armstrong and Ward (1926), and 'word group' by O'Connor and Arnold (1973).
2. Where '*tone*' is used in the sense customary in literary criticism, it is enclosed in inverted commas; *tone* is used without inverted commas when used in the phonetic sense.
3. Modernized spelling is used throughout these quotations.

LANGUAGE AS A LITERARY MEDIUM: AN UNDERGRADUATE COURSE

GRAHAM TRENGOVE

University of Aberdeen

In publishers' lists, in the proliferation of journals like *Language and Style*, and indeed in the present collection, there is clear evidence of the liveliness of academic interest in what practitioners of linguistics have to offer students of literature. Theoretical issues involved have been extensively debated if not resolved, and practical demonstrations of the virtues, or exposures of the limitations, of one approach or another have not been wanting. For several years now, English departments in some British universities have been seeking the best means to make their students aware of the potential rewards of systematically applying such linguistic knowledge as they have, or can readily be provided with, to the study of literary texts. One course with this purpose has been developed in Aberdeen, and has now been given since 1973. This essay describes that course, 'Language as a Literary Medium', its rationale and its syllabus, and goes on to consider whether it might usefully be adapted to the purposes of English departments in overseas universities.

The ultimate object of the course is to enhance students' critical understanding of literature and their ability to articulate it. To reach it we draw on a broader array of linguistic knowledge, ancient and modern, than is commonly brought into play in courses with titles like 'Stylistics', effecting a wish to integrate what is elsewhere often presented so as to appear discrete.

We start from the assumption that what a student first wants and is able to say about a poem, novel or play is, and should be, determined in large part by his personal response to it. In reading and coming to some understanding of a text, he has engaged in creative co-operation with the author, and needs (or may be required by his tutor) to share his perceptions and, we hope, his pleasure. However, this acknowledgement that literature speaks variously to different people and to successive generations is accompanied by our recognition that the reader, at least the undergraduate reader, should consider possible and probable original meaning, and by our belief that he can be brought to do so without necessarily falling victim to the intentional fallacy.

We offer help in a number of ways. First we demonstrate that subjective responses to a text flow certainly from linguistic choices made by the original author, but also from perceptions of those choices conditioned by the reader's own experience of the language of his time and, where relevant, of earlier periods. We seek to sharpen the student's awareness of the linguistic resources available to a writer, to reduce the constraints on this understanding set in particular by the process of unrecognized language change, and not least to provide him with a descriptive terminology and procedure which is useful because shared, but which is not elevated to the status of a critical dogma.

Most of the students for whom the course has evolved are primarily interested in literature and do not have an unlimited appetite for linguistic study. This restricts the proportion of their time which we can direct to language study of any kind and requires that our course design should highlight the practical benefits to their study of literature which we see as flowing from our approach. It also suggests to us a need to present this element of the degree course so that it is perceived by the students as central to their work. We indicate this to them in several ways. First, the paper for the course is one of the three which all students specializing in English must include among the total of eight which they offer at the final examination; it is not an option. Secondly, teaching for the course is undertaken, sometimes jointly, by lecturers whose primary interests may be either linguistic or literary or a combination of the two. This is intended to blur what has in some institutions become perhaps too sharply defined a boundary between 'lang.' and 'lit.'. Thirdly, lectures related to the course are distributed over 3 years, and for two of these are dovetailed into teaching which is otherwise mostly literary. These arrangements are not cynically cosmetic. They reflect our conviction that language study is beneficial to students of literature, but also our consciousness that this is not self-evident to people who have in their view conducted their studies quite successfully without this aid.

A base for the course proper is established during a one-year study of the English language conducted largely without reference to literature, though students normally follow a syllabus of literature as a concurrent but separate component of their work. This foundation year is also the necessary precursor to more advanced study of medieval literature, of the history of the English language, and of modern linguistics. It is meant to make possible an informed choice among these and other options open to students in the following years, and therefore includes components relating to each of them. We begin with 7 weeks' study of the structure of the modern language, including its phonetics and phonology. Then follows a brief treatment of the principles of historical and comparative linguistics as background to the historical study of English. The second terms begins with an intensive programmed course in Old English which is meant to enable students to read simple prose texts within 3 weeks. Thereafter the curriculum covers selected Old and Middle English texts, including some of the shorter Old English poems treated as literature, and the processes of language change reflected in them. The programme is completed by a survey of Scots, historical and contemporary. While each of these components has its own particular development in succeeding years, they are all seen additionally as making useful and different contributions to the study of language as a literary medium, which we take to be a proper approach to literature no matter what its date.

This is of course a crowded programme and the treatment of any one section is necessary limited. One consequence of this is that the description of the contemporary language is conducted in structural rather than transformational-generative terms, though the notion of syntactic transformations is informally introduced and used in practical exercises. The grammar used is an elementary form of Halliday's scale and category model, which, whatever its shortcomings for linguists, we have found sufficiently well adapted to the needs of our course, notably in encouraging students to perceive syntactic structures and to acquire a vocabulary with which to describe them. As only a small proportion of them arrive at university with much more than a fragmentary knowledge of traditional school grammar, it would be unrealistic to embark on the greater abstractions of generative grammar, at least in the time available. The consequent limitations on our freedom to refer to literary insights offered in transformational terms we have simply to accept.

On the other hand, the descriptive terminology developed in the 7 weeks devoted to the contemporary language is actively and consistently employed in lectures and tutorials through the year. Students are also constantly required to look at the different linguistic levels on which utterances or texts are organized. By the end of the year they should have the concepts and the vocabulary to allow them to recognize and discuss intelligently the phonological, syntactic, morphological, lexical and semantic aspects of any English text.

In the following 2 years we meet weekly in lecture or seminar and apply these skills to literary texts. Our first concern is to raise students' consciousness of, first, the effects of the passage of time on perceptions of literature, and, second, the literary effects possible at different linguistic levels. This provides a basis for the seminar discussions of short extracts from novels, poems and so on which in the later stages of the course become the prime focus of our efforts. In these discussions the accumulated information about the way English works now and has worked in the past is brought to bear on the internal features of the text and the way readers relate it to their experience of life and other literature.

The first stage of this programme lasts a year and includes a number of components. It begins with a series of lectures, nine in all, in which we demonstrate the consequences for readers of historical change in language, change in word meaning, in the vocabulary stock, in syntactic patterns, in pronunciation and in prosody. As themes these have already been touched on in the previous year's work; in this series the emphasis is on the elucidation of the probable intentions of the author given the date of composition, and on the removal of hindrances to comprehension raised by time.

This of course is the contribution made with varying degrees of effectiveness by the authors of critical editions but we feel that students ought to know something of the resources of linguistic scholarship drawn on by these editors. To this end, and because we wish to encourage students to be more than passive recipients of information, we ask them to investigate indicated aspects of brief selections of prose and verse from earlier periods, making use particularly of *The Oxford English Dictionary*. The exercise is so made that each student examines a different set of texts but each set includes instances of the same noteworthy linguistic features. Each student should thus have something separate to contribute to the seminars which occasionally replace the weekly lecture.

The second term begins with four lectures tracing the evolution, from the Renaissance to the early nineteenth century, in attitudes towards language, in beliefs about its nature, both as expressed by contemporary commentators and as reflected in the practice of writers of literature. The topics treated include the augmentation of the language from classical and foreign sources, the reaction against this, the consolidation of the vernacular language as the medium for learned purposes, the regularization of spelling, the development of poetic diction and the establishment of notions of correctness in grammar. As these are all familiar themes in the standard single-volume introductions to the history of the language, we take pains in lectures to show how a knowledge of them may improve our understanding of a play or poem, whether locally, explaining for example Shallow's comic admiration of Bardolph's fashionable use of 'accommodate' (*2 Henry IV*, III. ii.) or more generally in observing Shakespeare's recurrent and sometimes thematic references to the nature of language, as for example throughout *Love's Labour's Lost*.

These lectures themselves provide opportunities to counter the view that there has ever been only one kind of English, and they are followed by two lectures and two seminars of which the central purpose is to explore the multifarious ways in which language may vary in association with features of the context in which it is employed. Here are discussed the linguistic reflection of the age, the regional origin and the social background of language users, and also of the roles played by language users, their attitude to those they are addressing, the topics figuring in the exchange, the purposes with which those topics are raised, and the medium which is employed. This is an element which would fit as readily into the previous year's work on modern English were the time available, but it is not out of place here as it enables us to ask students to look closely at a wide range of Englishes without engaging in questions of literary merit. We present them with short representative texts taken from advertisements, insurance policies, public notices, travel literature, recorded conversations among friends or between shop assistant and customer, lectures, sports commentaries and reports, and so on. We ask first that the contexts in which the texts originally occurred be identified. This task successfully completed, as it invariably is by native speakers, we then require that they separate out the linguistic features which enabled them so confidently to name the context. Their first recourse is almost always to lexical features but they can be encouraged to pick out clues on the other linguistic levels. One way of doing this is to give out texts of the kind just described but in which all lexical items (as opposed to grammatical items like articles, prepositions and auxiliaries) have been replaced by the word-class labels *noun, verb, adjective* or *adverb*. Perhaps surprisingly the success rate for identification remains high, and, with prompting, students can often go a long way to reconstructing the original text. Ten or so fragments of about 50-100 words each provide ample material for a discussion which is meant to bring home to students of literature that the employments of English are many and diverse and by no means exclusively literary, to offer other ways of assessing style than on a scale 'good' to 'bad', and to promote the analysis of texts on all levels without engaging immediately in questions of aesthetic value. A valuable book to which we refer students in this connection is *Investigating English Style*, by David Crystal and Derek Davy (Longmans, 1969).

This divergence from orthodox foci of attention for an English department can only be brief, and in the last term of the year we return to what are unquestionably literary uses of English. However, we take care to include texts which drawn with varying degrees of obviousness on special varieties, or registers, of English not commonly associated in readers' minds with literature. This is meant to lend substance to the claim that in modern writing at least there are no limits on the linguistic resources which may be tapped for literary purposes. In this section of the course we consider fragments or paragraph-long extracts in which, successively, phonological, syntactic and lexical features can be seen as likely to trigger predictable responses from readers. One lecture and one seminar is devoted to each of these levels, this being our last major effort to persuade students that looking at the organization of texts at each different level separately can be a profitable stage on the way to comprehending the operation of the text as a totality. However, they are by this time, in our expectation and usually in fact, anxious to move on to a treatment of the texts which recognizes that devices on different levels work in relation with each other, perhaps to reinforce, perhaps to modify or subvert what would otherwise be their effect. Anticipating the work of the following year, we naturally encourage this tendency.

In the final year most of the teaching is done in weekly seminars, though these are interspersed with a few lectures. The focus of group discussion is one or two short poems or parts of poems, or extracts from novels, dramas, sermons or occasionally non-literally prose. Copies are given out well in advance and students are expected to come to the seminar able to relate their critical responses to aspects of the language used. They are expected to have identified any instances of historical linguistic change which may affect interpretation and hence perhaps judgement, in short to provide editorial glosses on linguistic points of literary interest. Even spelling might attract comment if it is evidently different to some literary purpose from the standard prevailing in the period of the work's composition, as it is for example in *The Rime of the Ancyent Marinere* (Coleridge's first version). They are also expected to have spent some time bringing to consciousness any patterns of repetition or variation in syntactic organization, vocabulary and sound structure, any notable divergences from or cleavings to expectations arising from their previous experience of language, whether literary or not, and any convergings or divergings of different linguistic devices, all this with an eye to the contribution made to their perception of the text as an organic unity. If at this point they still need reminding of the kind of observations that are likely to be interesting, they may usefully be referred to Geoffrey Leech's helpful *A Linguistic Guide to English Poetry* (Longmans, 1969).

The success of the seminar inevitably depends on the thoroughness of the participants' preparation, but, given that, it should be assured, without need for the promptings and constraints of a 'method'. If all present have previously sought to relate their feelings about the text to aspects of its language there should be no dearth of personal insights coming forward from people who ought by now to have the means to explain their origin and perhaps persuade others of their validity. As some guarantee that linguistic information proffered is accurate and that its literary relevance is properly weighed, these final-year seminars are jointly conducted by two tutors whose interests are complementary. We are fortunate at present in having enough willing language and literature tutors to allow the formation of several groups with no more than nine students in each. The potential danger that the voices of the tutors will preponderate has obviously to be guarded against but this requires only an extension of the restraint that a single leader of discussion needs to exercise. Given this framework and preparation, the discussion can be hospitable to matters of literary history, biographical detail, conventions of genre, social and historical background, and so on, without inevitably lacking discipline or losing coherence, because at any point the contributor may be asked to associate his comment with some observable feature of the text.

To meet the not unnatural feeling that there may be more to be learned from sitting back and listening to accustomed practitioners we offer in place of a formal lecture a public discussion of a short text undertaken by two lecturers in each of the remaining terms. Like the tutors for the seminars these lecturers represent the two contributing sectors of the department's expertise, but providing the discussion is not too carefully prepared in advance what happens is that they naturally take on each other's roles and speak from the kind of unified sensibility that they wish to encourage in their listeners.

This final-year programme also includes a number of lectures, not now a cohesive series, discussing different facets of language as a literary medium. Among these are treatments of individual writers which look at their use of language in particular poems or novels in relation to generalizations covering all their work. One seeks to give some impression of the importance of the long-lived tradition of rhetoric, its frequently unremarked survival in modern literature, and the possibility of talking about its uses without necessarily acquiring the one hundred plus terms which Shakespeare may be supposed to have had at his command. Another pursues a theme most recently and most comprehensively discussed in Norman Page's *Speech in the English Novel*, (Longman, 1973), that the simple distinction between the direct and indirect representation of speech, which is as much as is ever formally taught, is quite inadequate to account for the practice of English novelists, in whose writing students may learn to recognize and appreciate much subtle gradation between the orthodox possibilities. This lecture also embraces the closely related topic of the representation of thought in novels. Finally, the location of the university spurs our attention to the Scots and Scottish English varieties which so greatly contribute to the distinctive character of the literature of Scotland.

The seminar material is selected in more or less chronological order from the literature of the Renaissance to the present day. It is frequently though not invariably chosen so as to enable points made in preceding lectures to be pursued in discussion. So, a lecture on Milton is followed by a seminar perhaps comparing extracts from *Paradise Lost* representative of Satan's and God's utterances. Other meetings introduce topics not touched on earlier. In one we compare texts in which the language reflects an author's decision to work within a tradition with others in which it reflects an attempt to escape from pre-existing patterns and expectations. Linguistically experimental work such as that of concrete poets has proved a fruitful choice for another meeting, particularly in that attention is thereby drawn to the exploitation of the graphic form of language. A seminar in which we compare successive drafts of a text with its published form is especially valuable in persuading those slow to acknowledge the value of this approach to literature, because it is so easy to demonstrate the writer's own interest in decisions about what students may be inclined to regard as trivial matters of word order, punctuation, choice between words of similar meaning, and the like. From the extensive material readily available there is much to be said for choosing prose or poetry which is well known to those in the group, perhaps by heart. We have had success comparing the manuscript versions of William Blake's 'The Tyger' with the form printed in *Songs of Innocence and Experience*. This selection was suggested by E. W. Hildick's *Word for Word* (Faber, 1965) a useful collection of appropriate material especially for those without ready access to facsimile or variorum editions.

As recorded earlier, the course is separately examined in a paper which requires the demonstration in commentaries on short texts of the skills which the syllabus is meant to inculcate, and the display in essay form of knowledge of the linguistic background to literature acquired from lectures and suggested reading. This opportunity to monitor the course has given us some cause for satisfaction but has also indicated the need for minor adjustments in its design. We have for example increased the provision of seminars in the early terms to induce a more active engagement with the topics then introduced. Perhaps the most encouraging feedback comes from colleagues not directly involved in the course who claim to detect its benign influence in work done for them in other contexts.

Readers who have reached this point will no doubt have registered the omission of many aspects of recent work in linguistics which have been persuasively represented as in some way relevant to the study of literature. As has already been acknowledged, we do not, except in seminar asides, give any attention to insights offered by transformationalists. Equally, the promise apparent in discourse analysis, speech act theory, and the wider reaches of structuralism and semiotics remains unexploited in the planned work of the course, though again individual students may have their attention drawn to these developing areas. The reason is the simple one, now reiterated, that the course is designed for undergraduates, not all of whom readily accept that linguistic matters are central to their concerns, and who meet this approach to literature and have to find time for it as only one of many offered by the department.

The objects and syllabus of the course have been described so far mostly in terms of abstractions. To show what we are aiming for, we distribute to students a commentary derived from earlier discussions of *Macbeth*, I. vii. 1-28, and it may be helpful to incorporate it here.

> If it were done, when 'tis done, then 'twere well
> It were done quickly: if th'assassination
> Could trammel up the consequence, and catch
> With his surcease success; that but this blow
> Might be the be-all and the end-all here,
> But here, upon this bank and shoal of time,
> We'd jump the life to come. But in these cases
> We still have judgment here; that we but teach
> Bloody instructions, which, being taught, return
> To plague th'inventor: this even-handed Justice
> Commends th'ingredience of our poison'd chalice
> To our own lips. He's here in double trust:
> First, as I am his kinsman and his subject,
> Strong both against the deed; then, as his host,
> Who should against his murtherer shut the door,
> Not bear the knife myself. Besides, this Duncan
> Hath borne his faculties so meek, hath been
> So clear in his great office, that his virtues
> Will plead like angels, trumpet-tongu'd, against
> The deep damnation of his taking-off;
> And Pity, like a naked new-born babe,
> Striding the blast, or heaven's Cherubins, hors'd

> Upon the sightless couriers of the air,
> Shall blow the horrid deed in every eye,
> That tears shall drown the wind. I have no spur
> To prick the sides of my intent, but only
> Vaulting ambition, which o'erleaps itself
> And falls on th'other —

The syntactic choices we see Macbeth making here subtly contribute to the impression Shakespeare creates of a man perturbed by a commitment to an unambiguous assault on honour, legality and kinship which he can scarcely bring himself to acknowledge having made personally. In the opening sentence of the speech the action he intends is not given its customary name but rather referred to by the pronoun 'it', which has no overt antecedent, suggesting that Macbeth cannot easily bring himself to shape his thoughts to the reality of the deed. Additionally, this pronoun occurs as the subject of a passive verb in a sentence from which the agent has been omitted; the agent would of course have been a noun or pronoun referring to Macbeth, so that here may be seen another attempted evasion of the raw collocation of 'Macbeth' and 'murder'. Furthermore, the reiteration of the subjunctive forms 'it were done', "t'were well" indicates that he is trying to present the deed to himself as hypothetical rather than planned for imminent performance. Then the choice of the first person plural pronouns 'we' and 'our' in lines 7-12 also suggests a sought escape from personal responsibility. 'We' does not of course refer to a plurality of murderers-to-be but is rather to be read with generic meaning; it is an attempt to perceive what is uncomfortably personal as being universal instead, and thereby to anaesthetize his conscience. The occurrence of generic 'we' in the second sentence, beginning 'But in these cases . . .', is what might be called 'natural' in that a generalization about mankind is being made, but the subject of 'We'd jump the life to come' can only refer to Macbeth and is thus an instance of an 'unnatural' use of the generic which requires explanation of the sort proposed.

(Interpretation of it as an instance of the so-called 'royal we' seems inappropriate at this point.) It is noteworthy that Macbeth is not introduced unambiguously into subject position, whether as noun or pronoun, until line 13, in a sentence where he is contemplating the course of action which ought to be his if his monarch were to be threatened.

Lexical choices reinforce this pattern of psychological evasion. The latinate and polysyllabic 'assassination' (standing in sharp contrast with the almost entirely monosyllabic first line and a half, and with later words like 'bank', 'shoal' and 'jump') was very much more exotic a term in Shakespeare's day than now; indeed, this instance is one of the earliest occurrences of the word recorded in the *O.E.D.* It may reasonably be regarded as a euphemism for 'murder', or at least as lacking its bluntness. 'Surcease' in line 4, and 'taking-off' in line 20 are similarly indirect appellations for Duncan's proposed death. Macbeth uses the word 'murtherer' only in reference to an imaginary third party against whom he should defend Duncan.

Because of the processes of semantic development natural to language, it is necessary to gloss for modern readers a number of words in this extract, whether unfamiliar in form, such as 'trammel up', meaning to entangle in a net (as of birds) or hobble (as of a horse), or familiar in form but with a meaning different from those current now, here 'Faculties' in the sense 'powers', 'clear' in the sense 'free from guilt', 'striding' in the sense 'bestriding', and 'sightless', which means 'invisible'.

Ignorance of such developments may deny to the modern reader recognition of complex word-play such as that in lines 2-4, where 'consequence' may mean 'that which would follow' and also 'one of importance or rank'. Similarly, 'success', which is syntactically parallel with 'consequences', may be synonymous with it too, or mean 'prosperous issue'.

The semantic identity, on one reading, of the two components of these lines is reinforced by the markedly alliterative sound pattern operating within them which repeats /s/ and /k/ insistently. This is particularly to be noted in the phonetically closely similar 'surcease' and 'success', words which have it seems been deliberately juxtaposed by deviation from standard clause element order, which would be 'catch success with his surcease'. These two means of putting the words into conjunction make all the sharper the contrast in meaning; what is the end for Duncan is to be the beginning for Macbeth. The speed and finality of the act wished for by Macbeth is indicated by this stark tightening of the syntactic links between the words.

A combination of lexical and syntactic features operates to suggest that Macbeth is not being presented here as driven by ungovernable passion nor as emotionally torn between counter-acting desires. The syntax is, with sympathetic reading, remarkably clear; its patterns are those of carefully constructed argument, or controlled debate. The clause subordination shows above all an awareness on the speaker's part of reason and consequence; 'that' in lines 4, 8, and 25 means 'so that'. Words like 'first' (line 12), 'then' (line 14) and 'besides' (line 16) mark stages in an argument, whose grounds change considerably in the course of the soliloquy. The phrase 'in these cases' belongs to rational discourse; it is a means to generalization and consequently may be seen as another of Macbeth's evasions of the particularity of the intended murder. Inside the sentences syntactic clarity is the result of maintaining the standard order of clause elements Subject, Predicator, Complement; even the inherent mobility of the Adjunct element is little exploited here. The metrical line corresponds only infrequently with a major syntactic boundary, but this pattern of run-on lines suggests colloquial fluency rather than emotion-governed utterance.

Nevertheless, there is throughout the passage an undertone of emotional tension; anxiety is implicit in the metaphors 'trammel' and 'plague', in the boomerang rhetoric (traductio) of 'teach . . . taught', in the unusual collocation of 'bloody instructions', doubled in effect by being separated by the line structure from the verb of which it is the object. This bursts through to the surface in the hyperbolic energy of the complex of simile and metaphor in lines 19-25. 'Pity' is first anthropomorphized via the similes with 'babe' and 'cherubin', which suggest that grief is the innately natural and virtuous reaction to the deed, so that it can then be presented metaphorically as riding the wind. But then 'Pity' becomes the subject of the verb 'shall blow', so that 'Pity' is now identified with the wind; it blows the 'horrid deed', this implicitly like a speck of dust, into all men's eyes, their consciousness. Their reaction is so vigorous, the resultant tears from irritated eyes so copious and universal, that the wind is drowned. The violent transformations in this hyperbolic fantasy, perhaps apocalyptic in reference, represent Macbeth emotionally coming face to face with the true nature of his intentions. This is marked syntactically by the predictions rather than hypotheses carried in the indicative verbal groups 'will plead', 'shall blur' and 'shall drown'. Here his own proposed role is perhaps still not wholly in focus but the emphatic re-emergence of the first person pronouns in lines 25-26 marks the abandonment of evasion. Finally, the choice of the simple present indicative in 'o'erleaps' and 'falls' shows Macbeth acknowledging not merely that ambition, given certain conditions, *would* leap too far and so fall down on the other side of the cleared obstacle, but rather that ambition characteristically and inevitably *does* do this.

It need hardly be said that this presents a more consistent and coherent view of the speech than any that could emerge from a group and that the development of the argument is more ordered than it was, or could have been, in the circumstances of the seminar. However, as these are additional qualities that we hope to encourage in the written work of the individual student, we do not believe our editorial intervention to be inappropriate.

The group examination of the text was conducted in a loose to-and-fro of observation, hypothesizing, and search for confirmatory observation. To describe the procedure as a 'method' would be to claim too much, but there are some practices which we find helpful and do consistently follow, beginning with a reading aloud of the text. Then we make sure that the group takes into account possible changes of meaning in words or syntactic structures, changes in pronunciation, and the use of words or structures suggestive of some special variety of English. Thereafter tutors try to ensure that the discussion touches at some point on all linguistic levels on which the text may be eliciting some response. If necessary we do so by a bald injunction to look at, say, pronominal reference, but better by asking, as we did on the occasion recorded, whether there are any syntactic choices which reinforce lexical suggestions, already identified, of Macbeth's reluctance to confront the true nature of his proposed killing of Duncan.

If the view is advanced that this is nothing but practical criticism, we would acknowledge a family resemblance but we would point out that the discussion remains more closely and consistently attached to specified linguistic features than has usually been the case in work published under that banner. Additionally we would claim that it is informed by a more catholic understanding of the nature of the medium than normally seems allowed for in introductions to practical criticism, and that the preparatory work in the historical dimension of language study helps in the avoidance of the grosser clashes between authorial intention and subjective perception.

In our course we are looking not for arrivals at agreed destinations but for travel by fully logged routes. Hence, if the reading of the speech just proposed were to seem unsatisfactory to others, we would of course be open to other interpretations, always provided that they took more adequate account of all the linguistic features we have noted and sought to relate to the literary effects we perceive. To insist on our students' adopting this approach to texts and this response to interpretative argument from others, in at least a part of the work they do, seems to us a proper and necessary element of the department's demands on them.

Our own students are of course native speakers of English. We have now to consider what usefulness this course may have as a model for overseas university departments teaching literature to students for whom English is a foreign or a second language.

The evident differences between the teaching context for which the course was prepared and that for which it is now proposed seem to place considerable difficulties before those who might seek to introduce it. First, there is the undeniable fact that, even in overseas departments whose work can start from a foundation laid by many years of school preparation in English, the level of students' linguistic competence is rarely that of native speakers. This means among other things that they lack the experience of hearing and using a wide range of varieties, or registers, changing by the minute to suit the changing context which is part of daily life in any community. Or rather they lack this experience in English. However, they do have it in their native languages, and they do need to acquire it for English, both for their study of English literature, and for that everyday competence in the language that they will call on as tourists, business people, and the like. These two facts provide respectively a starting point and an incentive for the study of the varieties of English. Adjusting the course so that students first examine their adaptability in their own tongue would give them a realistic impression of their target. More time would probably have to be spent on this element of the syllabus but this does not invalidate the approach for an overseas department; it rather points to its relevance.

Because these students will by and large speak and write an English more flawed than that of native speakers, it may be supposed that they will therefore be inferior as commentators on texts. This does not by any means follow. On the contrary, it may well be that they are better placed than their British contemporaries in that they will almost certainly have studied the structure of English formally for much more time and in greater detail. They are consequently more accustomed to recognizing and discussing abstract linguistic features of English than are native speakers. In the experience of the present writer they are more likely to point out for example the apparently random changes between present and past tense that recur throughout Keats's 'The Eve of St Agnes'. On the other hand, they are usually less adept at perceiving the literary consequences of such devices. It is precisely the enhancement of the ability to do so that the course is meant to achieve. Again the aim of combining linguistic description and critical understanding remains good for the overseas context. The distribution of effort as between the two may be varied to take account of the relative strengths and weaknesses of the students.

Potential difficulties of a different kind may arise from a disparity in teaching and library resources as between the university where the course was evolved and those into which its introduction might be contemplated. There can be few overseas universities whose English departments do not employ language specialists, but, in some cases, their attention may be directed exclusively to the contemporary state of the language. Where this is so, the historical dimension of the course could not well be maintained, but the opportunity would remain for a fruitful conjunction of effort from language and literature specialists focused on texts drawn from the modern period. Inadequacies in library holdings of descriptive linguistic scholarship can be met, as they always have been, by dissemination of necessary information in lectures. If restricted funds were available to support such a course, they might best be used in improving holdings of dictionaries and grammatical descriptions of English. Perhaps the best investment of this kind is the purchase of the *Oxford English Dictionary*. In its photographically reduced two-volume format it comes within the reach of all but the most impoverished institutions, and the provision of several copies would not be an extravagance. As there exists no richer source of information about the medium of the literature they are reading it is most desirable that overseas university-level students should learn how stimulating consultation of this work invariably is.

The recurrent use of such scholarly tools can only have a beneficial effect on the students' language skills, and not only in the circumstances of the seminar. This claim may be made for the course as a whole; the convergence of linguistic and literary teaching produces benefits both immediately in enhancing students' personal interaction with novels, poems and drama, and, in the wider context, by extending their general linguistic competence.

It seems reasonable to suppose that sensitization to the manifold linguistic signals which combine to elicit responses in students as readers of literature will be reflected in their more effective and discriminating linguistic behaviour in all situations, academic and other. Herein lies the reward for the contribution of the language specialists. For the literature teachers satisfaction can be looked for in the greater personal involvement with literature which the course pattern allows and requires of the student. Insistence on the principle that reading literature is itself a creative endeavour, and that this process is a valid starting point for discussion of a text, seems likely to stimulate the active interest of overseas students whose acquaintance with English literature may not be extensive. It will anyway stimulate them more than the traditional prescription of literary history and received critical opinion, especially if the students' role is limited to the recording of information obliquely relevant to literary works they have not fully comprehended or perhaps not even read. Finally, the approach being advocated is salutory for students in that it retards their reaching conclusions about a text, and so helps to close off the easy exit from the text into the mechanical translation and subsequent contemplation of a second-hand version which hinder genuine study of a foreign literature.

Not least among the attractions such a course might have for an overseas department is its potential as a counter to the divergence of the many interests quite properly pursued within the ambit of English studies. This applies as much to the teaching staff as to the students. The design of the course calls for the concentration of many aspects of a department's expertise on to a common, limited target, and for this reason it should be a unifying influence. At the very least, participation in the joint leadership of seminars, where local resources allow this, may offer specialists the stimulus of a very different perspective from their own, and this in a frequently recurring situation where, like the students, they are bound always to associate any comment with some feature of the actual text. Our discussion has so far been largely conducted in perhaps indigestible generalities. The character of the approach described may emerge more persuasively if we employ it in respect of a brief passage from a modern novel.

> The Isle of Mugg has no fame in song or story. Perhaps because whenever they sought a rhyme for the place, they struck absurdity, it was neglected by those romantic early-Victorian English ladies who so prodigally enriched the balladry, folk-lore and costume of the Scottish Highlands. It has a laird, a fishing fleet, an hotel (erected just before the First World War in the unfulfilled hope of attracting tourists) and nothing more. It lies among other monosyllabic protuberances. There is seldom clear weather in those waters, but on certain rare occasions Mugg has been descried from the island of Rum in the form of two cones. The crofters of Muck know it as a single misty lump on their horizon. It has never been seen from Eigg.
>   It is served twice weekly by steamer from the mainland of Inverness. The passenger rash enough to stay on deck may watch it gradually take shape, first as two steep hills; later he can recognize the castle—granite 1860, indestructible and uninhabitable by anyone but a Scottish laird, the quay, cottages and cliffs, all of granite, and the unmellowed brick of the hotel. (Book 1, chapter 6)

In this section of *Officers and Gentlemen* (Chapman & Hall, 1955), Evelyn Waugh describes the approach of his protagonist, Guy Crouchback, to the remote island off the west coast of Scotland to which he has been posted for a period of commando training. The passage sets the tone for the part of the novel which it introduces, and conforms to the satirical note which is evident throughout, but much can be understood about its literary effect without reference to its context in the novel.

To perceive the extract as we may confidently claim Waugh expected native speakers to do, overseas students need first to recognize that many of its linguistic features are to be found together in a quite different context. If they have travelled for pleasure in the English speaking world, they will almost certainly have met the variety in which these features naturally occur. Even if they have yet to put their English to the test on this point, they may be referred to what will no doubt be comparable material in their own language.

For either group, a useful starting point is the sentence 'it is served twice weekly by steamer from the mainland of Inverness', which could have been lifted without a syllable being changed from a guidebook. The equivalent phrase in the student's first language will no doubt summon up for him an extensive set of associated idioms and vocabulary. This is equally true of the English phrase, and therein lies the source of the humour of these paragraphs, which can only be apprehended against the background of 'tourist' English. All the other sentences must be recognized as subtly amended standard components of a high flown and now old-fashioned guidebook account of the means of travel to, and points of interest in, no matter where Havana, Helsinki, or Haiphong. This is true of even the first sentence, in which humour issues from the negation of the underlying cliché of cut-price Baedekers, 'famed in song and story'. This insertion of a damaging negative is also exploited in rhetorical structures made equally familiar by use in such contexts. The third sentence takes the simple and well-known form of a summary list of notable sights, but the list puts a laird (Scots cognate of 'lord') into uneasy equivalence with a fishing fleet and an hotel as a tourist attraction; more risibly it ends with the anticlimactic 'and nothing more'.

The same device is used on a larger scale in the last three sentences of the first paragraph, which, while conforming to the tourist guide pattern of a description from a neighbouring vantage point, cumulatively expose the ill-favoured nature of the island's climate, recording with increasing bluntness the difficulties of observing it. The first suggests the affectedly learned vocabulary of the handbook author in its use of 'descry'. In contrast, the second wins comedy from the now unexpected occurrence of the word 'lump', whose banality and suggestion of a clumsy intrusion on the scene is completely out of key with its linguistic surroundings, especially with 'misty', the romantic euphemism which customarily conceals from prospective visitors to the area its meteorological shortcomings. These three sentences become progressively shorter and simpler, leaving the reader with the blunt and comically negative 'It has never been seen from Eigg'.

One of the pleasures offered by the passage is the delicately varied defeat of the linguistic expectations engendered by acquaintance with guidebooks. It would not be difficult to find one which coyly enjoins upon its comfortably-off readers the 'bold' step of savouring the approach to a new port from their steamer's deck. Here the replacement is of 'bold' by 'rash', similar but also crucially different in meaning, and thus a comically indirect pointer to the unfriendliness of the island's climate.

The subsequent catalogue of the components of the scene, as it would appear from a distant viewpoint supposedly occupied by the reader, is a rhetorical strategy which itself conforms to the stereotype guidebook style, but whose effect Waugh transforms. Each component mentioned is in itself an entirely probable feature of the landscape; each in turn is in one way or another made ludicrous. Given experience of the variety of English implicitly drawn on, we are in no way surprised to find the adjective 'granite' following 'castle' as one of the latter's identifying characteristics. Nor are we surprised to be told the date of its construction. But the lateness of that date is amusingly significant, revealing the castle to be only a Victorian reconstruction or confection, another product perhaps of the prodigal enrichment of the Highlands by romantic ladies. Similarly, the adjective 'indestructible' is common among the qualities attributed to ancient fortresses. Misled by the identical syntactic function and the morphologically and phonologically similar form of 'uninhabitable', the reader may not instantly recognize that the latter word does not figure in tourist prose and that it reflects a decidedly unromantic perception of the castle. The delayed recognition is comic, being analogous to the 'double take' of music hall and cinema usage. The satirical note is then confirmed by excluding from those who would find the castle impossible to inhabit only Scottish lairds, thereby categorizing them as other than normal human beings. Next, the alliterative linking of 'quay, cottages and cliffs' adds to the common and, as elsewhere employed, objective description 'all of granite' the suggestion of an oppressive overabundance of this rock. And lastly, the hotel, conspicuous enough as the solitary brick edifice in this granitic scene, is linguistically damned by the epithet 'unmellowed', a bruising negation of an adjective much favoured by those who paint word pictures of 'unspoiled villages nestling in the shadow of ancient oaks' and the like.

Thus in multifarious fashion, Waugh trades on a language variety whose lineaments he could be confident would be familiar to most of his readers. Of the other linguistic threads in the comedy which might be teased out, one might easily have been too broad had it not been for Waugh's restraint. Mugg, it may be necessary to explain to overseas readers, appears in no atlas of the British Isles, being the invention of the author. However, the name clearly echoes and combines those of the three genuine Scottish islands also mentioned, Rum, Muck and Eigg, which are English in sound but not in etymology. Their apparent collective absurdity invariably prompts amused disbelief from native speakers of English who have not previously encountered them, but Waugh recalls such reactions only indirectly, in the second sentence, when he invites his readers to consider the set of words with which Mugg rhymes, and in the fourth sentence, where he places last the extravagantly polysyllabic words so comically at variance with the expectations aroused by the standard guidebook locating phrase 'it lies amongst other . . .'. Similarly, though the ludicrous association of the island's name with the English word 'mug' are not to be overlooked, they are subtly attenuated by its spuriously Gaelic spelling.

There will be those who see this commentary as a ponderous attempt to explain a joke, a task which they regard as inherently foolish and doomed to failure. The present writer believes rather that to explore in detail how a text is perceived as humorous by a native speaker is only to pursue in a particular case the general and proper object of putting overseas students into closer connection with the English literature they study.

ON THE GOALS OF A READING PROGRAMME FOR STUDENTS OF ENGLISH AS A FOREIGN LITERATURE

KEITH JONES

The British Council, Germany

I want to argue that among the goals of an ESP reading programme aimed at preparing students overseas for the university study of English literature two are crucial. One is a set of interpretative conventions[1] and one is the use of certain rhetorical tropes.[2] In arguing for these to be given prominent consideration I shall idealize matters considerably by only focusing on preparatory requirements for the study of modern lyrical poetry and shall leave it to the reader to decide whether such goals would be valid for other genres.

Confronted with the text of a short poem such as *Ears in the turrets hear,*[3] a student with some basic competence in English is likely to need help from two sources. On the one hand he will need to know what are the basic ground rules for playing the literary interpretation game. What kind of activity is he engaged in? On the other hand he will need to know how to handle some of the detailed poetic effects of apparently unusual language realizations. What does this phrase or line mean or, rather, what can he get it to mean for him? In the second case he is confronted with the said, the actual choice of words of the poet, but what does the said say, what is the meaning of all these turrets and doors and locks and gables and disembodied eyes and ears? I shall argue that the second case is contingent upon the first and so let us look first at some of the conventions I have in mind.

1. The musical convention
   In poetry signifiers may be chosen for their fugal value, for the way they echo and modulate the sound values of other signifiers.

2. The animacy convention
   In poetry all signifieds are potentially carriers of consciousness, animate and articulate, so that stones speak to us as easily as Truth and tin drums, dragons and hawks.

3. The significance convention
   In poetry all signs that denote physical entities may be read as cues connoting moral values.

4. The coherence convention
    In poetry the linear sequence is motivated, juxtapositions are meant, no sign is redundant, and the whole is greater than the sum of its parts.

5. The plurality convention
    In poetry signs can be unpacked for the senses they connote and the associations they inspire. They offer journeys.

6. The literal convention
    In poetry all signifieds that may appear not to inhabit our everyday world may be read literally so that what changes in meaning is not words but the world. Poems make possible worlds.

7. The ellipsis convention
    In poetry what can be inferred may be omitted so that for wholes we may be given parts, for agents instruments, for the thing compared the comparison.

From these conventions[4] certain rhetorical tropes draw their values. Synecdoche (part for whole) and metonymy (e.g. agent for instrument) are resources enabling the practice of the convention of ellipsis while metaphor may realize the conventions of animacy, significance and plurality as well.

Let us now look at the process of reading from this perspective by considering the first four lines of the Dylan Thomas poem in a little detail.

Ears
How do we read this word? Synecdoche is a species of ellipsis, a convention whereby parts of a whole are presented as if the part were a whole, thereby achieving something akin to a close-up shot on film in that what is not shown is presumed to be there. But it is not only a part without its possessor, it is also vague. It creates an indeterminacy and provokes two things: the need for a reader to assign it a context as he encounters it and the subsequent need to check the appropriateness of that assignment. In Gricean[5] terms it is insufficiently informative and thus sets up an expectancy that more information will be forthcoming.

Ears in the turrets
Turrets denote small towers 'usually attached to a building, often containing a winding stair'.[6] But by the Convention of Significance any physical object may be granted a moral significance. The word stands for the small tower but what might the small tower stand for? We might recall how poets like Edwin Muir ('And Time locked in his tower') and Robert Browning ('Child Roland to the dark tower came') have established towers as symbolically resonant signs. Towers then are part of the symbolic currency of poetry. It is of course too early in the poem to know whether to invest in this kind of meaning if we are reading it for the first time, but the potential need for metaphorical inference is there.

Ears in the turrets hear

The musical convention of rhyme gives shape to the line by operating a kind of closure and doing so in parallel with the elliptical convention of metonymy. Metonymy, often conflated with synedoche, I shall gloss, after the manner of Schofer and Rice,[7] as being a convention for handling causation whereby, given the following pairs of terms — cause/effect, producer/product, agent/instrument, agent/action, instrument/action, one item of a pair may do duty for both, so a verbal realization of one conventionally implicates the others. Here the ears, the instruments of hearing, implicate some unknown agent or agents.

Ears in the turrets hear
Hands grumble on the door

Hands do not collocate with grumbling in accounts of general usage, and so accounting for this is perhaps doubly necessary for EFL learners. We have in fact a more stylish use of metonymy than before with the instruments of complaint achieving agentive effects. Metonymy is common in everyday discourse where the convention of ellipsis also applies as part of the general economy of language, but ellipsis is often pushed further in poetry so that some such sequence as 'hands knocking on door without finding a response begin to express the impatience of the person knocking in such a way as if he were grumbling at being denied entry' is condensed into four words.

In the second line all three elliptical conventions entwine in a coding which parallels the first line's and, in resonating thus with it, naturalizes its effects. The synecdochic effect (ears, hands), the metonymic effect (ears hear, hands grumble) and what I take to be the pure metaphoric effect, vehicles without specified tenors (turrets, door), compose an imaginary reality that the reader can sense but only arbitrarily depict. A situation has been constructed in ten words through conventions of suggestion that provides a frame of expectation, partly of a narrative nature, in that given this encounter — some presence in some structure perhaps under siege? — the reader awaits some outcome, and partly of a descriptive nature, in that given the visual vagueness of this encounter the reader's visual imagination awaits more detail, and partly of a symbolic nature, in that, given that the turrets and the door invoke a tower, the reader awaits the arrival of further cues to see what correspondences he might achieve on the moral plane. Thus is the reader drawn into the poem whose meanings he must co-produce.

Ears in the turrets hear
Hands grumble on the door
Eyes in the gables see
The fingers at the locks

Twentieth-century linguistics is premised on the assumption that the sound–sense bond of the sign is arbitrary but lyrical discourse can be seen as an attempt to 'motivate' that which in its origin was wholly 'unmotivated', as

Mallarmé has asserted.[8] For where the writer is concerned with creating an imaginary reality the process whereby signs are selected is motivated not by sense alone but by calling on sense/sound matrices so that at any point in the discourse choice is a function of the convergence of sense and sound possibilities. The context that emerges is partly a phonological context so that, as the lineal flow of the discourse goes under way, there is a persistent textural recursion whereby sounds are echoed and rhythms repeated as the poem anchors and reanchors itself in its phonological medium, in a way similar to the way conversation makes repeated reference to the tacit situation in which it is embedded. Being a unique construction, a poem always has to counter the reaction that its signs are arbitrary in a semantic sense, for a poem inherits no immediate context of situation.[9] A special case of the musical construction of context is syntactic parallelism, well exemplified in lines 3 and 4, varying as here from syntactic mimesis, as in line 3's syntactic mimicry of line 1, to a more allusive parallelism, as with line 4's syntactic echoing of line 2. A corollary of syntactic parallelism in particular, and the fugal nature of musical effects in general, is that the poem is persistently punctuated by moments of self-reference; these prevent it from being a rush to a destination outside the poem, though persistently referring the reader to the texture of the emerging object, through which attention to texture the reader is also constantly invited to reappraise the meanings he has assembled. In poetry there is a musical quest whereby both writer and reader are guided by where the patternings of sound take them: in rhyming the sounds of signs, the senses of the signs may meet to collude or collide. As *Octavio* Paz[10] asserts, in poetry signs talk to each other. In much of literary discourse the signs are like Chinese boxes that open to reveal other signs: thus in line 3 we open on line 1 and in line 4 we open on line 2. But it is not replicas we discover but growth. As we move on from the grumbling of hands to the picking of locks the parallelism and sound play amplify the narrative element of the expectation we have identified as the sense of a deliberate incursion into whatever meanings we assign to the tower. The amplification is a function of the elliptical tropes that both refine the sense of plot and increase its mystery, the use of synecdoche producing more precisely focused images (hands ⟶ fingers, doors ⟶ locks), the use of metonymy producing a second causal train (eyes – see, fingers – at) that is an effect of the first (hearing ⟶ looking, grumbling ⟶ lock-picking), and the use of pure metaphor naturalizing, legitimizing the symbolic resonance of 'turrets' by invoking 'gables', and 'doors' by invoking 'locks', thereby committing the reader to redouble his search for significance. And the product of this search at this stage of reading is for me the framing of a species of philosophical riddle, riddle in the sense that it is the job of philosophy to ask questions which have no single answer and which thus hide the answer necessarily because there is no single answer, a species of philosophical riddle rendered in the sensually allusive mode that lyric poetry has made its own. The riddle posed to me is that of the mind/body relation, the Cartesian crisis, a dramatization of the mind conceived of as in but not of the body but only able to mean through the body and so inevitably separated from other minds in other bodies, a theme at the heart of much twentieth-century literature with its consequences of the fact of loneliness and the difficulty of love, with an alienation that enables the consciousness to see the fingers at the locks but not feel them.

Shall I unbolt or stay
Alone till the day I die
Unseen by stranger-eyes
In this white house?

A sudden switch of perspective reframes and intensifies the theme of loneliness as the poem moves from depiction to dramatization, from scene to voice, from outside to inside, generating a new set of expectations and requirements, the expectations perhaps including some resolution of the dilemma of loneliness, the requirements including the achievement of coherence. Who is I? The mind we inferred from the ears and eyes of the first four lines! A mind or Mind? What is the white house? The white skin of the body that houses the mind? Just a white house? A house that is white because the body is innocent? What is being unbolted? Just the bolted doors of a white house? The psychological defences of a personality in retreat? The Cartesian prison? As we search for coherence the questions rise up multiplying indeterminacies, achieving plurality, but as they do so the musical strategy of rhyme and assonance — I, I, die, eyes, white, in one strand and stay, day, stranger in another — achieve a phonological cohesion among separated signs and the deft parallelism of

day I die
stranger eyes

holds together the middle lines of this four-line movement. This combination of under-determination of reference and over-determination of sound is of course one of the major semiotic strategies of lyrical discourse, a strategy that both creates message as object[11] to admire and message as labyrinth to wander in.

Hands, hold you poison or grapes?
The music limits the labyrinth. Why 'grapes'? Because it closes the stanza musically through the vowel harmony of gable, stay, day, stranger, grapes. Why 'hold you'? Because it enables the recurrence of hear, hands, hold. As a stanza unfolds phonetic freedom diminishes and sounds loop back. Just as the poet attempts to motivate his signs because ultimately the sound/sense relation is arbitrary so he attempts the effects of a fugue because ultimately language is linear.

Thus far our reading has shown how much interpretation seems to rely on:

1. The convention of ellipsis, not only because of the elegant economy of representation that can be achieved by synecdoche and metonymy but also because a sense of strangeness and narrative impulse is given by

the devices. Much of the effect of the first stanza comes from what has been omitted from the text but is nonetheless implied by it. A practised awareness of this convention and its attendant tropes would seem to be a pedagogic premise for our programme.

2. The convention of significance. Whether or not others will subscribe to my exact reading of the significance of turrets, doors, gables and locks, I would argue that to search for their significance via a metaphor that maps them on to a moral plane is a necessary interpretative procedure and one that gives the reader a point to his quest. Again a practised awareness of this convention and how it may be utilized by a pure species of metaphor — one that elides tenor and ground and only presents the vehicle — seems another certain pedagogic premise.

But the point of reading is ultimately not to decode but to experience. Ellipsis and significance of themselves are conventions that may turn poems into puzzles and reading into cryptography. Two of the other conventions we have invoked so far act as a necessary corrective:

3. The plurality convention.[12] The meaning of a poem being a text divorced from a physical context of utterance and an actual sender is not controlled by its author and the immediate environment and is thus irremediably plural given its elliptical coding and potential levels of significance. Its aim perhaps *is* to resonate in the memory, agitating associations and evaluations and producing a personalized meaning. Pedagogy should encourage this.

4. The musical convention. Part of the reading of poetry is surely to relish the musical experience so that sound patterns becomes not merely deft communicative means but also communicative ends in themselves. A pedagogic consequence of this would be coaching in the recitation of verse as well as analysis of poetic effect.

I take it as demonstrated that a practised awareness of the role of these four conventions should figure prominently among the goals of our reading programme and I should now like to take a closer look at the convention of coherence and how I see the poem as a whole cohering. Though the poem's theme is perhaps about states of mind, about conditions of loneliness, much of the poem is realized in terms of events that provoke the need to take decisions, and as such it has a strong narrative colouring. In the attempt to achieve coherence the poet can thus legitimately call on an aspect of literary tradition, the system of narrative conventions. How he calls on that tradition is his strategy and, as we shall see, he does so distinctively, in a way that defeats certain expectations, that transforms normal narrative conventions, that achieves style.

A useful characterizing of the structuring of narrative sequences is by Longacre.[13] He argues for the following perhaps classical sequence:

1. The Aperture. The conventional entrance into story through some such perspective as: Once upon a time . . .

2. The Setting. The main characters and principal locations are sketched in more or less detail.

3. The Inciting Moment. Some disturbance occurs to set the situation in motion.

4. The Developing Conflict. The disturbance becomes more critical, problems and complications becoming more involved.

5. Climax. The conflict reaches crisis proportions and the crisis intensifies until everything comes to a head.

6. Dénouement. Some happening or insight occurs that enables some resolution of the conflict to emerge as a possibility.

7. Final Suspense. Fresh complications frustrate resolution and narrative tension reaches its highest pitch.

8. Closure. Some resolution is achieved, whether happy or unhappy, whether comic or tragic, whereby some degree of equilibrium is restored.

The narrative sequence in the poem however seems to me to be structured as follows:

Movement — **Narrative value**

1. Lines 1–4 — The Inciting Moment
    Ears in the turrets hear
    Hands grumble on the door,
    Eyes in the gables see
    The fingers at the locks.
2. Lines 5–8 — The Developing Conflict
    Shall I unbolt or stay
    Alone till the day I die
    Unseen by stranger-eyes
    In this white house?
3. Line 9 — The Climax
    Hands, hold you poison or grapes?
4. Lines 10–14 — The Setting — widening focus
    Beyond this island bound
    By a thin sea of flesh
    And a bone coast,
    The land lies out of sound
    And the hills out of mind.

5. Lines 15–16   The Setting — narrowing focus
   No birds or flying fish
   Disturbs this island's rest.
6. Lines 17–20   The First Inciting Moment
   Ears in this island hear
   The wind pass like a fire,
   Eyes in this island see
   Ships anchor off the bay.
7. Lines 21–24   The Beginning of the Developing
   Shall I run to the ships   Conflict
   With the wind in my hair,
   Or stay till the day I die
   And welcome no sailor?
8. Line 25   The First Climax
   Ships, hold you poison or grapes?
9. Lines 26–28   Mixing the Inciting Moments
   Hands grumble on the door,
   Ships anchor off the bay,
   Rain beats the sand and slates.
10. Lines 29–31   Mixing the Phases of the Conflict
    Shall I let in the stranger,
    Shall I welcome the sailor,
    Or stay till the day I die?
11. Lines 32–33   The Climaxes as Closure
    Hands of the stranger and holds of the
       ships,
    Hold you poison or grapes?

In staging these movements of the poem into stanzas the poet has incorporated filmic devices as follows:

Stanza	Narrative Mode
1	Depicting the actual encounter
2	Flashback to setting
3	Flashback to anticipation of actual encounter
4	Cross-cutting between anticipated and actual encounter

The poet's strategy is a game with our expectations that seems to involve the following tactics:

a   frames within frames. Inside the frame of the lyric poem is a narrative frame and inside the narrative frame is a filmic frame, each frame[14] being by its very nature a structured set of expectations. The lyric frame is one where perhaps we do not immediately expect events strung out on a time dimension, the narrative frame one where we do expect events strung out on a time dimension, perhaps moving from aperture or setting to closure, and the filmic frame one where the time dimension is constantly being foreshadowed or dislocated in some way — techniques which have fed back into contemporary narratives in many explicit ways. Thus in beginning one's reading of the first stanza one rapidly senses a narrative thrust, an element of story in the poem, albeit realized in a highly elliptic way proper to poetry, but probably unusual in narrative prose, and one proceeds using lyric conventions to interpret the images and narrative conventions to interpret the succession of events. Then one encounters the second stanza, the value of which is difficult to perceive, for it does not follow on from the first stanza, and it is only when one reads it filmically as flashback that it coheres with the first. Similarly, as the labelling of movements and stages or stanzas alone makes clear, I trust, the whole reading of the poem is enriched if one appreciates the tactics of frame switching and mixing.

b   narrative transformations. In calling up narrative expectations and in opening the poem by plunging *in medias res* and moving from inciting moment to developing conflict in nine vivid suggestive lines the speed of the narrative thrust is such that we look forward to some dénouement. But the poet is playing the transformation game, the game of deletions and reorderings, and as there is no aperture so there is no dénouement, no final suspense, no usual sense of closure, these moves being deleted from the game; and the elements of narrative are not only subject to deletion but to reordering and to revaluing, reordering not only in the flashback-in-time sense in move 4 at the beginning of the second stanza but also to reordering of narrative logic, a principle of which is characterizable as

> *first* evoke the setting
> *then* bring in the disturbance
> *so* the rupturing of order is given impact

But the poet reorders this principle, first evoking the disturbance and then depicting the setting, a setting where hermetic seclusion is so complete that the irruption into it already portrayed is given extra impact. And in so reordering the sequence of expectations he obliges us to revalue what has gone before so that the narrative impulse of the first stanza is delayed but heightened by the second and further delayed by being replayed as if anticipated in the third. By the fourth stanza the tension generated by frustrated expectations of dénouement has thus been heightened and it is only in the fourth stanza's replay of the first and third that we realize that the point is that there is no dénouement because we are dealing in dilemmas, not in stories, and that the first stanza thus laid down the limits of the poem.

We have so far demonstrated five of our seven conventions, and to consider, briefly, the remaining two—the Animacy and the Literal Conventions—we need to turn to the Ted Hughes poem,[15] 'Prometheus On His Crag, 4,' which nicely illustrates their conjunction. For the poem to achieve its force our imaginations have to enter the world of myth, and as in a dream by Prometheus as the vulture rends him. Not to conjure the imagining is not to read the poem as experience but as text and as we argued earlier the whole point of poetry is to do both, and we may do it this way: we may use the text as instructions for assembling an imaginary reality and experiencing it as literal truth.[16] And granted this Literal Convention as the way into this poem we also grant the Animacy Convention whereby the feathers 'black, bold and plain' of the vulture each proclaim the vulture's message to Prometheus, not by implication but in actual literal black and white.

The contention then is that each of our seven conventions and the three tropes we have discussed are all crucial to the act of reading poetry and deserve prominence in any list of goals for a reading programme preparing students of English as a foreign literature. The conventions are crucial in that they constitute the ground rules of the actual language game of literary interpretation and the tropes are critical in that they constitute many of the moves in the special language game that is literary activity. But whereas the conventions could be said jointly to delimit the game of reading poetry the tropes are probably endemic in most discourse. And this provides a connecting link between the students' previous study of 'general' English and the special programme they would embark on. In early stages of our reading programme then the focus might be on tropes. A useful set of sensitizing exercises might begin by taking elementary items from the lexicon to show how their tropistic deployment has resulted in idiom and frozen metaphor.

Take **eye** for example and consider
1   eyeball to eyeball (*synecdoche* particularizing an encounter in almost cartoon fashion)
2   eye-sore: eye-opener (*metonymy* substituting effect for cause and implicating both)
3   eye-wash (*metaphor* transferring a physical process into a verbal process and adding *irony* on the way — i.e. that's clearing away what's right in front of your eyes, but it isn't rubbish, on the contrary . . .)

A second stage might involve taking images out of context and looking at them as metaphor in relation both to their syntactic form and musical appeal. Consider, from Ted Hughes,[17]
(1) wraith — rain (p.15)
(2) a sky dry as talc (p.149)
(3) the wind is inside the hill (p.22)
moving into more complex images
(4) If I wait, I am a castle
    Built with blocks of pain (p.144)
(5) Death is in the sperm like the ancient mariner
    With his horrible tale (p.114)
(6) The earth invalid, dropsied, bruised, wheeled
    Out into the sun,
    After the frightful operation (p.41)
and then the image as poem as in *haiku* and the imagists, at which stage a more thoroughgoing treatment of conventions might apply.

At such a second stage, writing exercises moving from prose comparisons through metrical and syntactic templates for images to handling the conventions of the *haiku* and the imagist poem would naturally form the bulk of classroom work, though almost as crucial would be the memorization and capable recitation of the *haiku* and imagist poetry that had served as models.

Given an imaginatively realized version of the first two stages so that lexical sensitivity, metrical sensitivity, musical conventions and basic species of metaphor, synecdoche and metonymy had come to be appreciated and were shown to be by virtue of memorization, recitation and creative writing exercises, then the programme could begin to tackle appropriate verse in an increasingly personalized fashion precisely because the students would be beginning to *handle* the conventions and resources of the special language activity they are to study. The extent to which our programme was an apprenticeship to a way of working with words would determine its success. For us perhaps as for Barthes[18] 'the goal of literary work (of literature as work) is to make the reader no longer a consumer, but a producer of text'.

Deciding on the goals of a programme is a complex and often highly circumstantial process involving institutional politics and many other socio-political variables. I have chosen to ignore these and to focus on arguing for a set of pedagogic premises that should form the basis of any design negotiation. The premises are these:
1. That any comprehension programme that takes a primarily formal approach to literary texts and largely confines itself to elucidating problems of syntax and lexis is bound to fail because it will be largely meaningless.
2. That what is basic to any act of interpretation is what kind of *activity* is going on in the social world of which it is a part.
3. That social activities are guided by sets of *conventions* often tacit, implicit, and assumed, and that this is true of the university activity of studying literary texts.
4. That in the special literary activity of studying modern poetry a set of some seven or so conventions are crucial in constraining and motivating what is a meaningful act of interpretation.
5. That by making these conventions explicit one is arriving at a set of interpretative strategies that variously enable the reader to decode texts and convert their potential imaginative impact into experience.
6. That these strategies both constitute a set of goals for our programme and inform its methodology particularly if certain key rhetorical devices are seen as embedded in these conventions.
7. That if we get the goals right then the methodology might reasonably follow always provided we have a properly participative methodology concerned with knowing *how* as well as knowing *that*.
8. That the key to a participatory methodology for our programme will be to balance expressive recitation and creative writing against more exegetical tasks so that, in an appropriately graded manner, the students personally experience the constraints and shaping functions of the conventions and tropes we have discussed.

Ultimately, ESP is English for social purposes, working with language to some end and by virtue of certain evolved conventions. We must thus base ESP programmes on some hypothesis about the social functioning of meaning in some particular domain. And that hypothesis needs to be one capable of being translated into an explicit pedagogy that students can come to appreciate and use as the basis for developing their own acts of judgement.

Ears in the Turrets Hear

Ears in the turrets hear
Hands grumble on the door,
Eyes in the gables see
The fingers at the locks.
Shall I unbolt or stay
Alone till the day I die
Unseen by stranger-eyes
In this white house?
Hands, hold you poison or grapes?

Beyond this island bound
By a thin sea of flesh
And a bone coast,
The land lies out of sound
And the hills out of mind.
No birds or flying fish
Disturbs this island's rest.

Ears in this island hear
The wind pass like a fire,
Eyes in this island see
Ships anchor off the bay.
Shall I run to the ships
With the wind in my hair,
Or stay till the day I die
And welcome no sailor?
Ships, hold you poison or grapes?

Hands grumble on the door,
Ships anchor off the bay,
Rain beats the sand and slates.
Shall I let in the stranger,
Shall I welcome the sailor,
Or stay till the day I die?

Hands of the stranger and holds of the ships,
Hold you poison or grapes?

Dylan Thomas

Prometheus On His Crag, 4

Prometheus On His Crag
Spotted the vulture coming out of the sun
The moment it edged clear of the world's edge.

There was nothing for him to do
As it splayed him open from breastbone to crotch
But peruse its feathers.

Black, bold and plain were those headline letters.
Do you want to know what they said?
Each one said the same:

'Today is a fresh start
Torn up by its roots
As I tear the liver from your body.'

Ted Hughes

References

1. See Jonathan Culler, *Structuralist Poetics: Structuralism, linguistics and the study of literature*, Routledge & Kegan Paul, 1975, ch. 8.
2. See Peter Schofer and Donald Rice, 'Metaphor, Metonymy and Synecdoche Revis(it)ed' in *Semiotica* 21:1/2, 1977.
3. Dylan Thomas, *Collected Poems*, Dent, 1952. See Appendix.
4. See Culler, *op. cit.* on conventions 3, 4, 5 and see Samuel R. Levin, *The Semiotics of Metaphor*, John Hopkins University Press, 1977, Part VII, on convention 6.
5. H. P. Grice, 'Meaning', *Philosophical Review*, 66, 1957; reprinted in P. F. Strawson, *Philosophical Logic*, OUP, 1967.
6. Chambers Twentieth Century Dictionary.
7. *op. cit.*
8. Cited in Fredric Jameson, *The Prison House of Language*, Princeton University Press, 1972, p.32.
9. See Henry Widdowson, *Stylistics and the Teaching of Literature*, Longman, 1975.
10. *Octario* Paz, *Alternating Current*, Wildwood House, 1974, p.4., 'Meaning does not reside . . . in what the words say, but in what they say to each other.'
11. See Pierre Guirand, *Semiology*, Routledge & Kegan Paul, 1975, p.7.
12. See Roland Barthes *S/Z*, Hill & Wang, p.170. trans, R. Miller, 1974. 'To interpret a text is not to give it a (more or less justified, more or less free) meaning, but on the contrary to appreciate what PLURAL constitutes it.' p.5.
13. Robert E. Longacre, *An Anatomy of Speed Notions*, Peter de Ridder, 1976, p.213.
14. See Erving Goffman, *Frame Analysis: An Essay in the Organization of Experience*, Harper & Row, 1974.
15. *Moortown*, Faber & Faber, 1979.
16. See Wolfgang Iser, *The Act of Reading: A theory of aesthetic response*, Routledge & Kegan Paul, 1978.
17. *op. cit.*
18. Barthes, *op. cit.* p.4.

LINGUISTIC APPROACHES TO LITERATURE: A SELECT BIBLIOGRAPHY

Compiled by Yolande Cantu
Literature Unit, British Council

Note: Only general works on discourse analysis, stylistics, etc., which expressly include discussion of literature or literary matter are included.

BAILEY, R. W. and BURTON, D. M. (1968) *English stylistics: a bibliography*, MIT Press, Cambridge, Mass.

BAILEY, R. W. and DOLEZEL, L. (1968) *An annotated bibliography of statistical stylistics*, Department of Slavic Languages and Literatures, University of Michigan: Ann Arbor.

GUIRAUD, P. (1954) *Bibliographie critique de la statistique linguistique*, Editions Spectrum: Utrecht and Antwerp.

HATZFELD, H. A. (1966) *A critical bibliography of the new stylistics applied to the Romance literatures, 1900-(1965)*, 2 vols., University of North Carolina Press: Chapel Hill. (University of North Carolina Studies in Comparative Literature, 5 and 37).

MILIC, L. T. (1967) *Style and stylistics: an analytical bibliography*, Free Press: New York; Collier-Macmillan: London.

Discourse analysis

BRAZIL, D. (1975–8) *Discourse intonation*, ed. R. M. Coulthard., 2 vols., University of Birmingham English Language Research: Birmingham English Language Research: Birmingham.

COULTHARD, M. (1975) *Discourse analysis in English: a short review of the literature. Language Teaching and Linguistic Abstracts*, 8, 2, April.

COULTHARD, M. (1977) *An introduction to discourse analysis*, Longman: Harlow.

DIJK, T. A. van (1977) *Text and context: explorations in the semantics and pragmatics of discourse*, Longman: London and New York.

FREEDLE, R. O. (ed.) (1977) *Discourse production and comprehension*, Ablex: Norwood, NJ.

FREEDLE, R. O. (ed.) (1979) *New directions in discourse processing*, 2 vols., Ablex: Norwood – see especially Vol. 2.

GRIMES, J. E. (1975) *The thread of discourse*, Mouton: The Hague & Paris. (Janua linguarum, ser. minor, no. 207).

HARRIS, Z. S. (1963) *Discourse analysis reprints*, Mouton: The Hague. (Papers on formal linguistics, no. 2).

Literary stylistics

AKHMANOVA, O. S. (1976) *Linguostylistics: theory and method*, Mouton: The Hague and Paris. (Janua linguarum, ser. minor, no. 181).

BABB, H. A. (1972) *Essays in stylistic analysis*, Harcourt Brace: New York.

CHAPMAN, R. (1973) *Linguistics and literature: an introduction to literary stylistics*, Arnold: London.

CHATMAN, S. (ed.) (1971) *Literary style: a symposium*, (International Symposium on Literary Style, 1969), Oxford University Press: London and New York.

CHATMAN, S. and LEVIN, S. R. (eds.) (1967) *Essays on the language of literature*, Houghton Mifflin: Boston and New York.

CHING, M. K. L., HALEY, M. C. and LUNSFORD, R. F. (eds.) (1980) *Linguistic Perspectives on Literature*, Routledge: London.

CLUYSENAAR, A. (1976) *An introduction to literary stylistics: a discussion of dominant structures in verse and prose*, Batsford: London.

CRYSTAL, D. and DAVY, D. (1969) *Investigating English style*, Longman: London.

DARBYSHIRE, A. (1971) *A Grammar of style*, Deutsch: London.

DIJK, T. A. van (ed.) (1976) *Pragmatics of language and literature*, North-Holland Publishing Co.: Amsterdam & Oxford.

DIJK, T. A. van and PETOFI, J. S. (eds.) (1977) *Grammars and descriptions.* de Gruyter: Berlin and New York. (Research in text theory, no. 1).

DILLON, G. L. (1978) *Language processing and the reading of literature: toward a model of comprehension*, Indiana University Press: Bloomington and London.

DRESSLER, W. U. (ed.) (1978) *Current trends in textlinguistics*, de Gruyter: Berlin and New York. (Research in text theory, no. 2).

EATON, T. (1966) *The semantics of literature*, Mouton: The Hague and Paris.

EATON, T. (1972) *Theoretical semics*, Mouton: The Hague and Paris.

EDWARDS, P. (1968) 'Meaning and context: an exercise in practical stylistics'. *English Language Teaching*, *22*, 3, pp.272–7.

ENKVIST, N. E. (1973) Linguistic stylistic, Mouton: The Hague.

ENKVIST, N. E., SPENCER, John and GREGORY, M. J. (1964) *Linguistics and style*, Oxford University Press.

ENKVIST, N. E. (1975) *Style and text: studies presented to Nils Erik Enkvist.* Editorial committee: Hakan Ringbom et al., Skriptor: Stockholm; Åbo Åkademi: Abo.

EPSTEIN, E. L. (1978) *Language and style*, Methuen: London.

FOWLER, R. (ed.) (1966) *Essays on style and language: linguistic and critical approaches to literary style*, Routledge: London.

FOWLER, R. (1971) *The languages of literature: some linguistic contributions to criticism*, Routledge: London.

FOWLER, R. (1975) *Style and structure in literature: Essays in the new stylistics.* Blackwell: Oxford. (Language and style, no. 16).

FOWLER, R. (1966) *'Linguistics, stylistics, criticism?'. Lingua* (Amsterdam), *16*, 2, April, pp.153–65.

FOWLER, R. (1972) *Style and the concept of deep structure, Journal of Literary Semantics* (The Hague), 1, pp. 5–24.

FREEMAN, D. C. (ed.) (1970) *Linguistics and literary style*, Holt, Rinehart and Winston: New York.

GALPERIN, I. R. (1977) *Stylistics.* Higher School Publishing House: Moscow, 2nd ed. rev.

GARVIN, P. L. (trans. and ed.) (1958) *A Prague School reader on esthetics, literary style, and structure.* American University Language Center: Washington D.C.

GRAUSTEIN, G. and NEUBERT, A. (1979) *Trends in English text linguistics*, Zentralinstitut für Sprachwissenschaft Berlin.

GUIRAUD, P. and KUENTZ, P. (1970) *La stylistique: lectures.* Klincksieck: Paris. (Initiation à la linguistique, ser. A, 1).

GUTWINSKI, W. (1976) *Cohesion in literary texts: a study of some grammatical and lexical features of English discourse.* Mouton: The Hague, Paris.

HALLIDAY, M. A. K. and HASAN, R. (1976) *Cohesion in English*, Longman: Harlow. (English Language ser. 9).

HASAN, R. (1967) 'Linguistics and the study of literary texts', *Etudes de Linguistique Appliquee*, 5.

HENDRICKS, W. O. (1976) *Grammars of style and styles of grammar*, North-Holland Publ. Co.: Amsterdam.

HIATT, M. R. (1975) *Artful balance: the parallel structure of style*, Teachers College Press, Columbia University, New York and London.

HILL, A. A. (1965) *Essays in literary analysis*, [No publisher] Austin, Texas.

KACHRU, B. B. and STAHLKE, H. F. W. (eds.) (1972) *Current trends in stylistics*, Linguistic Research: Edmonton. (Papers in Linguistics, Monograph ser. 2).

LEECH, G. N. (1970) 'The linguistic and the literary'. *Times Literary Supplement*, 23 July, pp.805–6.

LOTMAN, J. (1975) 'Notes on the structure of a literary text', *Semiotica* (The Hague), *15*, 3, pp.199–205.

LOTT, B. (1960) *Style and linguistics: an inaugural lecture delivered in the University of Indonesia on 31 October 1959*, Djambatan: Djakarta.

MILES, J. (1967) *Style and proportion: the language of prose and poetry*, Little, Brown: Boston.

MOODY, H. L. B. (1970) *Varieties of English*, Longman: London — see especially Part II.

MOWATT, D. A. and DEMBOWSKI, P. F. (1965) 'Literary study and linguistics', *Canadian Journal of Linguistics*, *11*, 1, pp.40–62.

OHASI, Y. (1978) *English style: grammatical and semantic approach*, Newbury House: Rowley, Mass.

PEARCE, R. (1977) *Literary texts: the application of linguistic theory to literary discourse*, University of Birmingham English Language Research: Birmingham. (Discourse analysis monographs, 3).

PERSSON, G. (1974) *Repetition in English*, University of Uppsala; distributed by Almqvist and Wiksell. (Studia Anglistica Apsaliensa, 21).

PRATT, M. L. (1977) *Toward a speech act theory of literary discourse*, Indiana University Press: Bloomington.

SEBEOK, T. A. (ed.) (1960) *Style in language*, Technology Press of MIT; Wiley: New York.

SOPHER, H. (1976) 'Stylistic analysis of literary material', *English Language Teaching Journal*, *31*, 1, pp.63–71.

SPENCER, J. W. (1964) *Linguistic and style*, Oxford University Press.

THORNE, J. P. (1970) 'Generative grammar and stylistic analysis', in Lyons, John (ed.), *New Horizons in Linguistics*, Penguin: Harmondsworth.

TURNER, G. W. (1973) *Stylistics*, Penguin: Harmondsworth.

UITTI, K. D. (1969) *Linguistics and literary theory*, Prentice-Hall: Englewood Cliffs, N.J.

WIDDOWSON, H. G. (1974) 'Stylistics', in Corder, S. Pit and Allen, J. P. B. (eds), *The Edinburgh course in applied linguistics*. Oxford University Press.

Application of linguistics to particular genres

BENNET, W. A. (1977) 'An Applied linguistic view of the function of poetic form', *Journal of Literary Semantics* (Heidelberg), *6*, 1, pp.29–48.

BURTON, D. (1980) *Dialogue and discourse: a sociolinguistic approach to modern drama dialogue and naturally occurring conversation*, Routledge: London.

CHATMAN, S. (1973) *Approaches to poetic*, Columbia University Press: New York.

CHATMAN, S. (1965) *A theory of meter*, Mouton: The Hague, London.

CULLER, J. (1975) *Structuralist poetics*, Routledge: London.

FOWLER, R. (1977) *Linguistics and the novel*, Methuen: London.

GENETTE, G. (1980) *Narrative discourse*; trans: by Jane E. Levin; foreword by Jonathan Culler, Blackwell: Oxford.

HESTER, M. D. (1967) *The meaning of poetic metaphor: an analysis in the light of Wittgenstein's claim that meaning is use*, Mouton: The Hague and Paris.

LEECH, G. N. (1969) *A linguistic guide to English poetry*, Longman: London.

LEVIN, S. R. (1962) *Linguistic structures in poetry*, Mouton: The Hague.

LODGE, D. (1966) *Language of fiction: essays in criticism and verbal analysis of the English novel*, Routledge & Kegan Paul: London; Columbia University Press: New York.

PAGE, N. (1973) *Speech in the English novel*, Longman: Harlow.

PERRINE, L. (1976) *The art of total relevance*: (papers on poetry), Newbury House: Rowley, Mass.

Statistical studies

AITKEN, A. J., BAILEY, R. W. and HAMILTON-SMITH, N. (eds.) (1973) *The computer and literary studies*, Edinburgh University Press: Edinburgh.
DOLEZEL, L. and BAILEY, R. W. (1969) *Statistics and style*, Elsevier: New York.
LEED, J. (ed.) (1966) *The computer and literary style: introductory essays and studies*, Kent State University Press: Kent, Ohio. (Kent Studies in English, 2).
WISBEY, R. A. (ed.) (1971) *The computer in literary and linguistic research: papers from a Cambridge symposium*, Cambridge University Press. (Publications of the Literary and Linguistic Computing Centre, University of Cambridge, 1).
WILLIAMS, C. B. (1970) *Style and vocabulary: numerical studies*, with a foreword by Randolph Quirk, Griffin: London.
YULE, G. U. (1944) *The statistical study of literary vocabulary*, Cambridge University Press. Third International Symposium on the Use of the Computer in Linguistic and Literary Research, *The computer in linguistic and literary studies*, ed. Alan Jones and R. F. Churchouse.

Semiology

BARTHES, R. (1967) *Elements of Semiology*, Translated from the French — Jonathan Cape: London.
ECO, U. (1979) *The role of the reader: explorations in the semiotics of texts*, Indiana University Press: Bloomington and London. (Advances in semiotics).
HAWKES, T. (1977) *Structuralism and semiotics*, Methuen: London.

Teaching

DOUGHTY, P. S. (1968) *Linguistics and the teaching of literature*, Longman: London. (Nuffield Programme in Linguistics and English Teaching, paper 5).
KAPLAN, R. B. (1972) *The anatomy of rhetoric: prolegomena to a functional theory of rhetoric: essays for teachers*, Center for Curriculum Development: Philadelphia. (Language and the Teacher, 8).
RODGER, A. (1969) 'Linguistics and the teaching of literature', in Fraser, H. and O'Donnell, W. R. (eds.), *Applied linguistics and the teaching of English*, Longman: London.
WIDDOWSON, H. G. (1975) *Stylistics and the teaching of literature*, Longman: Harlow.

Some traditional approaches to style

BROOKE-ROSE, C. (1958) *A grammar of metaphor*, Secker and Warburg: London.
EMPSON, W. *Seven types of ambiguity*, Chatto and Windus: London.
HOUGH, G. (1969) *Style and stylistics*, Routledge: London.
NOWOTTNY, W. (1962) *The language poets use*, University of London Athlone Press: London.
STEINER, G. (1972) *Extra-territorial: papers on literature and the language revolution*, Faber: London.
ULLMANN, S. (1963) *Language and style: collected papers*, Blackwell: Oxford.
ULLMANN, S. (1973) *Meaning and style: collected papers*, Blackwell: Oxford.

Periodicals

Journal of Literary Semantics: An International Review, Mouton: The Hague, 1972–75; Julius Groos: Heidelberg, 1977.
Language and Style: An International Journal, City University of New York, Queen's College Department of English, Queen's College Press: Flushing NY, 1968.

Lingua e Stile, Il Molino: Bologna, 1966.
Poetica: An international journal of Linguistic-Literary studies, Shuban International: Tokyo, 1974.
Style. University of Arkansas, Department of English: Fayetteville, 1967.
Travaux de linguistique et de litérature, Editions Klincksieck: Paris, 1963.